Assessing the Language of Young Learners

British Council Monographs on Modern Language Testing

Series Editors: Barry O'Sullivan and Vivien Berry, both at The British Council

This series – published in cooperation with the British Council – provides short books in the area of language testing. These titles are written by well known language testing scholars from across the world and members of the British Councils' Assessment Research Group (ARG). The books offer both a theoretical and a practical perspective to language testing and assessment – proposing, where required, models of development, which are reflected in actual test tasks. They are unique in that they are co-authored by individuals with considerable academic experience teamed with those with equally considerable teaching and assessment experience, thus offering the reader a unique insight into the link between theory and practice in the area. In many, though not all, cases, the books illustrate their approach with reference to actual test items, from the British Council's Aptis test service.

Forthcoming:

Assessing Language on the Global Stage: The British Council and English Language Testing, 1941-2016
Barry O'Sullivan and Cyril Weir

Assessing the Language of Young Learners

Angela Hasselgreen and Gwendydd Caudwell

SHEFFIELD UK   BRISTOL CT

Published by Equinox Publishing Ltd.

UK: 415, The Workstation, 15 Paternoster Row, Sheffield, South Yorkshire, S1 2BX
USA: ISD, 70 Enterprise Drive, Bristol, CT 06010

www.equinoxpub.com

First published 2016

British Library Cataloguing-in-Publication Data
A catalogue record for this book is available from the British Library.

Library of Congress Cataloging-in-Publication Data
Names: Hasselgreen, Angela, author. | Caudwell, Gwendydd, author.
Title: Assessing the language of young learners / Angela Hasselgreen and Gwendydd Caudwell.
Description: Sheffield, UK ; Bristol, CT : Equinox Publishing Ltd, [2016] | Series: British Council monographs on Modern Language Testing | Includes bibliographical references and index.
Identifiers: LCCN 2016009766 (print) | LCCN 2016023310 (ebook) | ISBN 9781781794692 (hb) | ISBN 9781781794708 (pb) | ISBN 9781781794760 (e-PDF) | ISBN 9781781794777 (e-epub)
Subjects: LCSH: Language and languages--Ability testing. | Language and languages--Evaluation. | Language and languages--Age differences. | Second language acquisition--Ability testing.
Classification: LCC P53.4 .H38 2016 (print) | LCC P53.4 (ebook) | DDC 407.6--dc23
LC record available at https://lccn.loc.gov/2016009766 ISBN: 978 1 78179 469 2 (hardback) 978 1 78179 470 8 (paperback)

ISBN: 978 1 78179 469 2 (hardback)
         978 1 78179 470 8 (paperback)

Typeset by CA Typesetting Ltd, www.sheffieldtypesetting.co.uk
Printed and bound in the UK by Lightning Source UK Ltd., Milton Keynes and Lightning Source Inc., La Vergne, TN

Contents

List of Figures

List of Tables

Preface

Children and teenagers – the subjects of this book – have to be handled with care. This is particularly true where assessment is involved, which can have a major impact on the learner, whether in the case of a 'high-stakes' test or an everyday classroom interaction. Ensuring that this impact is maximally positive in the assessment of the second or foreign language (L2) of young learners involves considerable knowledge and expertise.

We need to know and understand something of the learners themselves: how they develop socially and cognitively, and what they are capable of linguistically, as demonstrated in their first language (L1). We need to know what is reasonable to expect that they can 'do' in an L2, and how proficient they have the potential to become. We need to know about assessment itself: how this may be carried out and used in the process of learning, and how tests, which play such a significant role in assessment for all purposes, can be made and used in a principled way. For the results of assessment to give us detailed and useful knowledge, we need an insight into what makes up different aspects of language use, such as speaking or vocabulary. And crucially, we need to recognize that 'young learners', defined here as being from about five to 17 years, consist of a large and diverse collection of individuals, and that the child at one end of the young learner spectrum is a very different learner from the teenager who will emerge at the other end, a decade or so later.

This volume draws on the authors' many years of experience in the field, as well as a realization that many issues, such as those described here, still need to be looked into and clarified. In an attempt to do this, we have separated the young learner group into three broad age ranges – younger children (5/6 to 8/9 years), older children (8/9 to 12/13 years) and teenagers (12/13 to 17 years). With these three groups in mind, the book sets out to answer a series of questions, which can be summed up below.

- What are the social and cognitive characteristics of each group, and how are these manifested in L1 development?
- How can these maturity factors constrain what can be expected in L2 ability and use?
- Is there any correspondence between the levels in the Common Euro-

pean Framework of Reference for Languages (CEFR) and what can be mastered at the three stages defined here?

- How might principles of assessment, specifically relating to the concepts of formative assessment and testing, be applied to young learners as they mature?

What emerges from this initial investigation is then applied, in turn, to the testing of reading, writing, speaking, listening and vocabulary and grammar. Theoretical models of these constructs are drawn on to establish what is involved in 'performing' in the L2. For each age group, an analysis is made of the characteristics of testing each of these skills. Examples from tests are used to illustrate these characteristics. A series of tables is finally presented, summarizing the cognitive, social and language development for each age group and the general implications of these for L2 testing.

The book is intended for a wide readership. The underlying questions, findings and conclusions from the study can be of interest to those involved in either research or practice, in the fields of assessment or teaching of the L2 of young learners. They may hopefully be tempted to look further into some of these issues in more depth. It is also hoped that the concrete and practical nature of this book will provide support to practitioners in many of the decisions they make – often on a daily basis – when assessing the L2 of their learners. We do not pretend to provide all the answers, but are confident that we may, at least, have gone some way towards clarifying issues at the heart of this important, challenging and often delicate area of assessment.

Introduction

Young learners are different from adults, in both their maturity and, to a large extent, their world. School is the most normal arena for language learning, and frequently also for language use. Young learners are defined here as children from about 5 years to 17 years; the younger the learners, the more 'different' they are. By considering them in a series of age groups – younger children (5/6 to 8/9 years), older children (8/9 to 12/13 years) and teenagers (12/13 to 17 years) – this book sets out to examine how age can affect learners' ability to perform in a second or foreign language (L2), and how this impacts on assessment.

We begin, in Chapter 1, by looking at developmental issues, with a focus on first language (L1) development in children and teenagers, allowing us to see possible linguistic limits of young learners at different ages. Chapter 2 moves the focus to the L2, defined here as any language acquired other than the L1, or mother tongue(s). The chapter investigates the knowledge and skills needed to communicate in the L2, and the domains of L2 use, and how these are influenced by developmental factors. In Chapter 3, the Common European Framework of Reference: Learning, teaching and assessment (CEFR) (Council of Europe 2001) is discussed. This document, although drawn up with adult learners in mind, is increasingly at the heart of what young learners learn, and how they are assessed. We examine the levels of the CEFR, and look for any possible correspondence between the different levels and what young learners are capable of in their L2. We also note some shortcomings of the CEFR for use with young learners. What emerges from this is drawn on in the later chapters, where actual assessment is studied.

Chapter 4 introduces L2 assessment. The notions of formative and summative assessment are discussed, and some important principles of both classroom assessment and testing are presented. Testing is highlighted as the central theme of what follows in the book, but this is not to the exclusion of formative assessment. Testing can be as much a part of everyday classroom assessment as of formal examinations.

The remaining chapters focus on testing: what we test, how we test it and how we judge performance – from young children to teenagers. The age-related conclusions from Chapters 1 to 3 on developmental issues, language ability and domains, as well as the findings relating to the CEFR levels, are all drawn on here. The 'four skills' – reading, writing, speaking and listening – are dealt with in Chapters 5 to 8, with a theoretical model of each skill being presented as the basis for analysing actual testing, across the various age groups. The order in which the skills are examined is primarily related to the simplicity of structuring the chapters, and will be returned to in the discussion of these chapters. Chapter 9 veers from the default, communicative type of testing, by briefly considering the testing of vocabulary and grammar.

It may be surprising to some that we are treating 'skills' separately in this way. With the increased use of the Internet and social media, the boundaries between reading, writing, speaking and listening are rapidly becoming fuzzier. Our writing is increasingly interactive, often in the form of 'chatting'. We may use internet-based programmes such as Skype not only to talk, but to read or work together on documents. However, there is still a need among teachers and others dealing with young people, to know how well they write, speak or understand what they read and hear. It is important to know how to assess these, and get some kind of profile of the performance of our learners.

To conclude, it should be mentioned that while English is the L2 referred to in almost all the examples of research and testing in this book, there is no reason why this information should not, in principle, apply to other L2s. It should also be acknowledged that the two authors have wide personal experience with the assessment of the language of young learners, both in Norway and in countries where the British Council has been active in language testing. This means our familiarity with the subject encompasses quite a large part of the world; it also means, however, that the reader must bear with us when noticing that many examples are taken from our own work and research with the young learners we have grown to be most concerned for. Young learners tend to have that effect!

1   Children and Teenagers: Developmental Issues

Regardless of how young learners perform in an L2, we can be fairly sure that they are relatively competent in their L1. As they develop cognitively and socially, so their L1 will expand. In this chapter, we will briefly outline some findings on cognitive and social development, before examining how this development is manifested in the L1 of children and teenagers as they mature. We will also look for trends in the development of L1 literacy. Only by equipping ourselves with some knowledge of L1 development will we be in a position to make claims about what children and teenagers can be expected to acquire and do in an L2.

Cognitive and Social Development

The work of Piaget (e.g. 1926) has had a great influence on current beliefs about the way children and adolescents develop cognitively, i.e. in their thinking. Piaget identified four distinct stages of development, which can be summed up as:

1. *Stage 1 (0 to 2 years): Sensori-motor stage* (characterized, for instance, by repetitive movements like kicking, reaching out for and looking for things, and imitating).
2. *Stage 2 (2 to 7 years): Pre-operational* (characterized, for instance, by egocentrism, and a very limited attention span).
3. *Stage 3 (7 to 11 years): Concrete operational* (characterized, for instance, by the development of logical thinking, in a 'concrete' way, an increasing attention span and decline in ego-centricity).
4. *Stage 4 (11 to 12 years and beyond): Formal operational* (characterized, for instance, by the ability to think logically and systematically on abstract matters).

This four-stage model has been criticized on several grounds, including: that Piaget's experiments have been found to be flawed; that children are not believed to move in a straightforward way, from stage to stage; that cultural factors have been found to affect cognitive development; and that this development does not cease around 11 to 12 years, but has been found to continue into adulthood (Pinter 2011). Furthermore, the work of Vygotsky (e.g. 1978) has been influential, maintaining that the stage at which a child can perform an operation cannot be considered as a point, but rather as a zone (The Zone of Proximal Development), and within this zone the child's ability to perform is dependent on the degree of support s/he receives through interaction. Clearly, there are also considerable individual differences in development, making it difficult to predict the age at which a child may reach a particular stage.

However, the notion persists that 'something happens' in the development of children and adolescents, which manifests itself in distinct advances in cognitive and social development around the lower and upper ends of primary school, as well as into and beyond puberty. This is supported by findings on spurts in brain growth during childhood and the teenage years (Morgan 2013; Pinter 2011; Epstein 1986). Moreover, Piaget's stages, if not the actual ages assigned to them, are reflected and further built on in research findings in a wide range of aspects of cognitive and social development, many of which have been found relevant to the acquisition and assessment of language, both L1 and L2.

Drawing on works such as Morgan (2013), Pinter (2011), Nippold (2006), McKay (2005), and Cameron (2001), the following rough stages can be identified in the development of aspects such as memory (storage and recall), understanding and verbal reasoning, social development and self-perception, attention span, and the kind of tasks which are 'doable'. It must be emphasized that the ages associated here with these stages cannot be regarded as more than approximate, owing to the influence of both individual and cultural/contextual factors.

Younger children (roughly up to 8 to 9 years) have a limited short-term memory and attention span and may have difficulty carrying out tasks which require attending to several things at once. They see the world with a simple 'unaffected' eye, and do not have concepts organized into more adult categories (such as hierarchies, for example fruit/banana), which can affect their approach to certain tasks, as well as the speed of recalling things. They are learning about the world through concrete experience, and can best perform tasks which draw on their personal knowledge. They are beginning to form friendships, but are still very adult-dependent. They tend to have an exaggerated sense of what they are able to do. They have a great need for fun, play and fantasy.

In *older children* (roughly from 8 to 9 up to 12 to 13 years), the speed of recalling and processing information begins to increase rapidly. Children at this stage start to organize concepts into categories, and can cope with more abstract ideas. They can solve simple logical problems, and carry out more complex tasks, appreciating 'wholeness' in tasks which involve coherent parts. They are gradually moving from being dependent on adults to their friends and peer groups, and are learning to cooperate and collaborate. They are developing a more realistic sense of what they know and can do.

In the teenage period (13 to 17 years), the ability to form the gist of large amounts of information, and to sort essential ideas from non-essentials, develops. The understanding of cause and effect emerges, together with a more complete notion of time. Abstract problems can be tackled using logic. However, in their early teens (13 to 15 years) forming opinions and problem-solving are still reliant on real-life experiences, and world knowledge often remains limited. Peers tend to be more influential, and easier to talk to, than adults, while self-esteem tends to drop.

Even in the later teens, brain development continues. Morgan (2013) cites research which shows that, in adults and children, brain activity in interpreting emotions and in decision-making takes place in the prefrontal cortex, which governs rational decisions. In the teenage brain, this activity moves to the amygdala, which is associated with emotion and gut reactions – instinct rather than logic. This can be an explanation for the volatility of teenagers and their difficulty in, for instance, reading the faces of adults around them (Morgan 2013: 33). While this shift of activity is taking place, grey matter is growing rapidly and branch-like synapses are being formed.

Morgan goes on to describe three stages of adolescence, as the brain continues to develop. In early teens (roughly 13/14), this more volatile behaviour prevails and potentially bad decisions are made, being governed by the amygdala. After an initial spurt of growth, the synapses start to be pruned back and reason returns (roughly 14/15), so that teenagers then start to take an interest in those around them and become more self-aware, potentially recognizing previous bad decisions. Additional skills start to be developed in the approach to the final stage (15 to 17 years): jokes can be better understood, information linked more easily and apparently opposing ideas reconciled. An appreciation of deeper meanings and literature is developed, as are the teenagers' own beliefs (2013: 183). Thus, teenagers go through different stages, which can affect their interpretations of situations they are in or their reactions to them. Moreover, their self-awareness increases as they get older, along with their ability to interpret higher-level and wider aspects of the world around them.

First Language Development

While any clear link between developmental factors and the acquisition of a learner's L2, which is subject to numerous contextual variables, would be very difficult to establish, it is reasonable to suppose that the way a first language develops is closely related to cognitive and social development. Moreover, an insight into what is typically mastered in an L1 at a particular age range can, at least, provide us with an upper limit for what we can reasonably expect of an L2 learner of the same age.

Nippold's (2006) meta-analysis of an extensive body of research, carried out on the acquisition of L1 English from childhood to adulthood provides just such an insight. She presents research findings on the acquisition of a wide range of linguistic abilities, which together give a colourful and detailed picture of the gradual mastery of language, which continues well into and, in many aspects, beyond the teenage years.

The most salient of these research findings on *the lexicon, figurative language, discourse and pragmatics*, and *syntax* are presented in some detail below. All references in this discussion are to works cited in Nippold (2006). For an overview of Nippold's findings on attainment at ages 5, 10, 15 and 25 years, see Appendix A.

The Lexicon

During school years, the lexicon is believed to increase by around 2000 to 3000 words per year, or 5 to 8 words per day (Nagy and Scott 2000). The way in which words are understood has also been found to progress steadily; young children understand the physical meanings of words, but not until about 11 or 12 years can they be expected to clearly understand figurative meanings alongside the physical, for example *bright,* according to Asch and Nerlove (1960). Adverbs of likelihood and magnitude, such as *probably* and *rather*, only begin to be mastered around 10 years, according to Hoffner, Cantor and Badzinski, (1990). Nippold, Ward-Lonergan and Fanning (2005) maintain that abstract nouns show a clear development after about the age of 11, and into adulthood. The greatest development in derivational morphology (i.e. the use of affixes, such as *un-* or *-ness*) is claimed to take place between about 9 and 14 years, according to White, Power and White (1989). The ability to recognize the meaning of morphologically complex words has been found to correlate with reading ability throughout the school years and beyond by Mahony (1994), and Carlisle (2000).

Figurative Language

The research evidence on the development of using and understanding figurative language, such as idioms, metaphors, jokes, slang and sarcasm, suggests that the ability to produce and understand these increases during school years (Morgan 2013), but the difficulty of these varies greatly with the familiarity, concreteness or transparency of the individual item, according to Evans and Gamble (1988). Douglas and Peel (1979) maintain that common transparent idioms can be understood by young children, while even adults may struggle to understand some of the more low frequency and opaque ones. The ability to fully understand sarcasm, particularly when accompanied by intonational clues, steadily develops from about 11 years, according to Capelli, Nakagawa and Madden (1990).

Syntactic Attainment

The development of syntax, in both written and spoken language, has been found to be very marked during the school years. This applies to both intra-sentential (within sentences) syntax and intersentential (connecting sentences) syntax (Karmiloff-Smith 1986).

At its most simple, intrasentential growth can be seen in the length of sentences or spoken utterances, which is frequently measured in terms of the number of words in a C-unit (communication unit) or T-unit (terminable unit) (Loban 1976), or in the mean length of utterance (MLU) (Leadholm and Miller 1992). Each of these units consists of a main clause plus any modifiers, such as subordinate clauses. There is a steady increase in the mean length of these units through the school years and beyond, although genre also affects this length. Average T-unit lengths have been found to be greater in persuasive writing than in descriptive, which in turn are greater than in narrative, regardless of age (Crowhurst and Piche 1979). Intrasentential growth is also characterized by a gradual increase in the range of conjunctions used, such as *when, and,* or *both,* as well as in the full understanding of many of these. *Although* and even *but* have been found to be little understood around the age of 6, and not fully understood even by 12 years (Katz and Brent 1986). Intersentential growth is observed through the increased use and understanding of adverbial conjuncts, such as *furthermore* and *however.* Children generally master a very limited range of these, and their development only really takes off in adolescence and continues into early adulthood, according to Scott (1984). This has an effect on the ability to write in genres such as persuasive or argumentative, which particularly depend on these conjuncts (Crowhurst 1987).

Discourse and Pragmatics

Findings on the development of discourse and pragmatics here focus on: conversation, narration, persuasion, negotiation and explanation. The focus here is on spoken discourse. The development of written discourse in children is less predictable, being bound up with the degree of their literacy, which will be the subject of the Literacy Section.

Studies on conversation show a refinement from childhood to adulthood in a range of elements. Brinton and Fujiki (1984) investigated the conversational skills of 5 year-olds, 9 year-olds and young adults. They concluded that there was little development between 5 and 9 in the ability to stay on topic, to produce extended dialogue, or to shift smoothly between topics, in contrast to the adults. However the 9 year-olds produced more varied, less repetitive utterances than the 5 year-olds. A marked increase during adolescence in conversational coherence – staying focused on what had been introduced, adding relevant information to the topic and showing awareness of what others thought – was found by Dorval and Eckerman (1984). Moreover, in a study by Larson and McKinley (1998), adolescents were shown to be clearly more relaxed and to produce better conversational performances on a wide range of indicators when talking to their peers, than when talking to unfamiliar adults.

Narrative is a genre familiar even to most pre-school children, who can often produce their own stories. Stein and Glenn (1979) examined the use of 'story grammar' (including setting, characters, episodes, initiating event, attempt to solve a problem, consequence and internal (emotional) responses of the characters) in re-telling stories. Little difference was found between 7 year-olds and 10 year-olds on all elements of story grammar except on internal response: the 10 year-olds were better able to recall the feelings and desires expressed in the story. The age-related use of cohesive devices such as conjuncts (see the discussion earlier) has also been shown to manifest itself in story-telling ability (Nippold 2006: 274–75).

In persuasion, a major development from childhood to adolescence appears to be the extent to which the listener's perspective is taken into account, for example, as shown in Piche, Rubin and Michlin's study (1978), where 10 year-olds and 15 year-olds were compared.

The ability to negotiate has been shown to develop markedly in adolescence and beyond, as maintained by Selman, Schorin, Stone and Phelps (1983). Again, greater social and other awareness appears to be a major factor, along with more fully-developed powers of verbal reasoning.

The development of explanation is illustrated by studies using 'giving directions' and explaining games. In giving directions, 7 year-olds, 10 year-olds and adults were compared by Lloyd (1991). The 10 year-olds and adults were shown to be more precise than the younger children, and more likely to 'get their listener' to the location than the 7 year-olds. The adults, however, used more terminology (for example *left*, *straight on*), and were more efficient, using fewer, more compact terms. Nippold, Hesketh, Duthie and Mansfield (2005) studied explanation of games in participants of 8, 11, 13, 17, 25 and 44 years, allowing them to choose their own game or sport, and measuring the explanations in t-units. A steady progression was found across the entire range, which was conceded to be a possible result of greater topic knowledge.

Literacy

While the term 'literacy' can be used to refer to having knowledge or skills in a wide range of contexts, for example, computer literacy or assessment literacy, it will be used here in its rather traditional sense of the ability to read and write. Literacy and language development are inextricably bound together. Language proficiency is basic to what we can read or write, while what we meet in print has a great effect on our language development.

Just as L2 language development cannot reasonably be expected to progress beyond the stage reached in the first language development, it might also be assumed that literacy in the L1 is a presupposition for L2 literacy, an issue which will be taken up in Chapter 5. But while it is possible to posit age-stage relationships in L1 development, as shown above, such a relationship in the case of literacy is far less straightforward. Put simply, while virtually everyone masters an L1 in some form, there are many who never learn to read and write. And even in societies where attending school from early childhood is the norm, defining literacy at any particular age is fraught with difficulty.

Where stages of literacy linked to age ranges are identified, for example in McKay (2005) and Nippold (2006), these tend to be based on what is generally expected by society, and what students are required to do as they proceed through schooling. McKay cites Puckett and Black's (2000) table of 'widely held expectations of literary development', which can be summed up as follows:

- 5 to 7 years: learning the basics of how reading and writing work; developing a basic vocabulary to enable slow and deliberate reading.
- 7 to 9 years: beginning to understand how reading and writing are used; developing an increasingly large sight-reading vocabulary (i.e. automatic recognition of whole word); gradually managing to read silently, as well as aloud with some fluency and expression.
- 9 to 11 years: expanding thinking through reading and writing; increasing the reading vocabulary and the speed and fluency of reading; adjusting to different purposes of reading.
- 11 to 13 years: continuing to expand thinking through reading and

writing and to increase the reading vocabulary and the speed and fluency of reading; spending more time reading a variety of fiction and non-fiction; beginning to understand that there are different ways of interpreting text.

(Adapted from McKay 2005: 21)

Nippold's conclusions on the stages of development of literacy typically attained across a range of ages add detail to what is involved in literacy (adapted from Nippold 2006: 22–23 and Appendix 16.1), and can be summarized as follows:

- 5 years: sight-reading a few common words; identifying words that rhyme; writing some names of family members; understanding simple stories read aloud.
- 10 years: decoding thousands of words; reading quickly and accurately; reading for pleasure, knowledge and learning about the world; using morphological analysis to decode unfamiliar words; being challenged by inferential and theme comprehension; writing effectively in narrative and descriptive genres; learning to spell morphologically complex words.
- 15 years: critically evaluating texts, recognizing conflicting viewpoints and distinguishing fact from fiction; spending less time reading for pleasure and more time reading for school work; writing longer essays using literate words; using morphological knowledge to spell difficult words.

When (and if) individuals reach these stages, and the extent to which they acquire the skills involved, are influenced by many factors. It is well documented that the home environment, including socio-economic factors, access to books and being read to at an early age, has a great and often long-lasting impact on literacy. Hartas (2011) makes a link between parental involvement in supporting children's learning at pre-school age and reading achievement around adolescence. Allington (2015), in his study of the problems associated with literacy in the middle school years in the USA, cites poverty as going hand-in-hand with dropout rates in later schooling, which in turn are closely associated with struggling to read in third grade. Allington laments the sad record of reading achievement in US schools, where two-thirds of eighth-graders (aged 13–14) have been shown to read below the expected proficiency level needed to perform most tasks at that grade. In investigating causes, he lays much of the blame at the door of the schools and curriculum writers, and particularly the 'one-size-fits-all' approach, whereby everyone in a grade is required to share a common degree of literacy. Students are frequently overwhelmed by texts that are simply beyond them, either because the language is too advanced, or because they lack the background knowledge necessary. This often has disastrous results for literacy and educational achievement in general, perhaps highlighting the danger of putting too much trust in the kind of age/stage descriptions of literacy shown above.

Adolescence seems to be a particularly critical period regarding literacy. Allington (2015: 76) cites a study of 2007, which alarmingly revealed that US adolescents report that they spend less time reading than readers in any other age group, either younger or older. This is reflected in the findings of a study by Van Schooten, de Glopper and Stoel (2004), who showed a decline in Dutch students' attitudes to reading, as well as in the frequency of reading books from grades 7 through 11 (cited in Van Gelderen, Schoonen, Stoel, de Glopper and Hulstijn 2007: 487).

A study of adolescents' attitudes to reading by Conradi, Jang, Bryant, Craft and McKenna (2013) cites a number of factors which influence adolescents' opting to read and their engagement in reading. These include their perceptions of themselves and their identities as readers, their role in choosing what to read, and whether their friends and family are readers.

To round off this section, let us take a look at a piece of writing by an 8 year-old, shown in Figure 1.1.

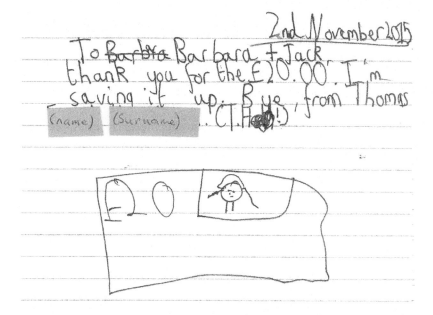

Figure 1.1: A thank-you letter by an 8 year-old (L1)

This is a fairly standard thank-you letter to an aunt and uncle for a birthday present. It was written with no help. The handwriting is good, the sentences well constructed and the spelling perfect. All of the essential 'bits' are there, including the date. Yet, unmistakably, this is a child's letter. The clues come not in the basic language, but in the choices Thomas has made, with elements such as *To* Barbara and Jack, *£20.00*, the full name signature (blanked out here) with initials in brackets, and of course the picture of the £20 note! These are signs that the emergence of knowing what is appropriate to a genre happens only gradually in children – which is why their writing is so delightful!

Conclusion

This chapter has outlined aspects of the development of children and teenagers which seem salient to the main theme of this book – the assessment of the L2 of young learners. Stages in development have been described, which can shed light on what we may justifiably expect of the L2 language ability of learners at different ages, as well as on how we can go about assessing this.

Cognitive/social development was considered first, presenting a rough characterization of children and teenagers across a series of stages. This has relevance for aspects of the tasks we can give learners at different stages, such as the degree of attention the task requires, the demands on memory, the complexity of the thinking involved and the abstractness of the concepts involved, as well as such considerations as whether or not support might be given, whether self-evaluation can usefully be used, or, in a spoken task, who the interlocutor should be, in order to ensure optimal performance.

Next, L1 development was considered. Here, a range of findings from Nippold's (2006) meta-analysis of L1 developmental research were presented in some detail, with a comprehensive overview of findings related to a series of ages presented in Appendix A. The detailed nature of our presentation is justified by the fact that what is of interest is not so much general underlying traits, but how these are manifested in the actual language which children or teenagers appear able to master. The findings presented here involved the development of the lexicon, syntax, figurative language and discourse, specifically conversation, and narrative, persuasion, negotiation and explanation.

Finally, the discussion moved to literacy. Of the three aspects of development discussed in this chapter, literacy is the one most subject to environmental factors, even leaving aside cultures where schooling and literacy are not taken for granted. Where stages of literacy have been identified, such as those presented here, it is difficult to know how far the perception of these is shaped by what typically goes on in the classroom. Added to this, there are a wealth of studies which have shown the extent to which an individual's literacy can be either fostered or hampered by environmental conditions, for example, relating to the family, the peer group or, indeed, the classroom itself. So, the question can be posed as to how the understanding of literacy presented here can have relevance for the assessment of L2 in young learners. Firstly, the stages presented can act as a rough guide when designing tasks involving the written language for specific age groups. Secondly, the great individual variation in literacy, throughout childhood and teenage years, means that those involved in making assessment tasks should, as far as possible, cater for a wide range of abilities in reading and writing, and avoid drowning young people in heavy, uninspiring texts. Thirdly, and perhaps most importantly, it has to be acknowledged that any assessment of the written language, may reveal more about literacy than L2 competence. This should be taken into account when interpreting and acting upon a low assessment result, and highlights the importance of assessing both the spoken and the written language.

The insight gained from these findings can inform us of the kind of language/discourse we can reasonably expect our learners, across a range of ages, to be able to produce or understand. This is of significance to the content of assessment tasks, as well as to criteria and feedback. The remaining chapters will all build, to some degree, on what has emerged in this one.

2 The L2 of Young Learners

Having probed into the development of young learners, and how this is reflected in what they can do in their L1, we will now turn to what is most salient to this book – the L2 of young learners. We cannot tie actual stages of L2 development to ages, as this is affected by contextual factors, such as how old learners are when they meet the L2. However, by knowing something about what they are typically able to do in the L1, we are better able to judge what is reasonable to expect that learners of certain ages are *potentially* able to do in their L2, which is the subject of this chapter.

By L2 we mean a language acquired other than the L1 or mother tongue(s), and the term will be used whenever it is unnecessary to distinguish between specific types of L2, such as second, foreign, third or additional language. The fundamental ability required to master the L2 should not, on the whole, be affected by any such distinction. It is important to recognize, however, that issues of whether the L2 is being taught as a foreign language in school, or is the language of mainstream teaching, and/or whether it is a language used outside school, may all have a considerable effect on the uses learners will be required to put their language to, and on the way it develops.

It is well established now that knowing an L2 refers to knowing how to use it in communication, rather than simply to having a head full of linguistic facts. The ability to perform in the L2 is often termed 'communicative language ability' (e.g. Hasselgreen 2004). In the first section of this chapter, we will consider what we mean by communicative language ability, and how the age of the learner may impact on this. We will then consider the domain, or area, of language use, and how this may be described for young learners in different age ranges.

Communicative Language Ability/Knowledge

Because communicative language ability and the knowledge required for this are two sides of the same coin, we will use both terms here, depending on our focus. Since the 1970s, many attempts have been made to define just what is meant by communicative language ability (for example, Hymes

1972; Canale and Swain 1980; Bachman and Palmer 1996). The models that have emerged vary mainly in the way different abilities are grouped, this often depending on how the model would be used, for example in teaching or testing. What seems commonly acknowledged, however, is a perception that in addition to the basic language 'bits' – such as sounds, words or basic grammar required to communicate an idea – we need a number of other kinds of ability and knowledge. For instance, we need to understand how a text is given structure and coherence, and how it fits into the wider context. A 'text' here means (based on Carter and McCarthy 2006) any piece of language written or spoken that is coherent and, in itself, carries some real meaning. It can be as long as a novel or as short as the word 'stop!'. It is at least as important to know how to take turns in a conversation as to be able to write a formal letter. We also need to know what the appropriate way of expressing something is in a particular culture or context. In England, it is important to know that 'See you later' is not a commitment to a plan, but a friendly way of saying goodbye among young people. And, in getting off a bus in some parts of the country, it is normal to thank the driver, and considered a breach of etiquette not to. We also need strategies to keep the communication on track, despite potential problems.

These different types of ability or knowledge can be summed up as a four-part model of communicative language ability (CLA), adapted from Hasselgreen (2004).

1. *Microlinguistic ability:* The ability to understand and use, with some degree of correctness, the basic 'building blocks' of language, such as vocabulary, syntax, sounds, and spellings.
2. *Textual ability:* The ability to create or understand coherence in a spoken or written text, for example, through the use of connectors, or through structures or routines associated with different genres and types of spoken discourse.
3. *Sociolinguistic ability*: The ability to adapt language to the way that it is typically used or expected in the particular situation or cultural group.
4. *Strategic ability*: The ability to use various devices to keep the communication going, in the face of difficulties, and to check for and tackle potential breakdowns in communication.

This model is a simplified version of many of the models it is related to, such as that of Bachmann and Palmer (2010), who, for example, place *strategic competence* separately from *language knowledge* in their model. Bearing this in mind, and not regarding our model as 'written in stone', it will be used here because it is practical, and not unwieldy to apply. Moreover its components, while not independent of each other, can be identified through indicators in the actual language produced or processed.

Let us now consider the young learner, and the extent to which s/he can be expected to demonstrate these abilities in the L2. Clearly this is, to a large extent, dependent on the level of proficiency of the learner, regardless of age; a 6 year-old 'near bilingual' will manage much more than an adult beginner in a language. Just how a young learner of any age acquires the L2 and the factors that affect this acquisition are complex issues, which will not be discussed here. What will be of concern here is how the age/maturity of a learner can constrain the development of CLA, and this will be discussed in the light of what has been presented in Chapter 1 on cognitive/social development and L1 (English) development.

Microlinguistic ability in a child, in terms of vocabulary, morphology and syntax, is limited. Only gradually are abstract nouns, and words involving concepts not in the child's personal experience, acquired. Morphology and syntax, including the use of suffixes/prefixes, conjunctions and adverbial conjuncts linking sentences, which can place demands on verbal reasoning, cannot be expected to develop fully before the teenage years. A study by Hasselgreen and Moe (2006) of the use of conjunctions in the L2 English writing of Norwegian pupils reflected this development, showing a marked increase in range used from age 12/13 to 15/16 years, when pupils rated as being on same CEFR levels (A2 and B1) were compared. It is interesting to note, incidentally, that acquiring the sounds of a language does not appear to be age-dependent, as is clear from even the language of babies. Studies such as Tahta, Wood and Loewenthal (1981) suggest that in the case of replicating the sounds of an L2, younger children are, at least, not disadvantaged by age.

Textual (or discourse) ability is largely subject to the restraints on microlinguistic ability shown above, as well as on emergent genre and discourse skills. In the L1, narrative skills are shown to emerge in very young children, and stories, descriptions and very simple explanations are frequently worked-with genres in the L2 primary school classroom. Conversational skills exhibited in younger children develop rapidly from adolescence, while some genres, such as persuasion, may not be fully mastered by young adults. Cekaite's (2007) study of L2 Swedish of 7 to 10 year-old immigrants showed that basic conversational skills can be successfully acquired through classroom interaction. Hasselgreen's (2004) study of 14-15 year-old Norwegians demonstrated that, in turn-taking in conversation, these students used appropriate markers such as *well* and *okay*, although with limited ranges compared to native speakers of the same age.

Regarding written texts, maturity in, for example, verbal reasoning and the awareness of others' perspectives, might be expected to accompany familiarity with an expanding range of genres. As shown in Figure 1 in the previous chapter, Thomas' letter (L1) exemplified how even the genre of a thank-you letter may only be acquired gradually. Studies such as Gebhard and Harman (2011) emphasize the need for L2 learners to be explicitly taught an understanding of genre use, in order to reach their full potential. It should be added that textual ability also involves an understanding – in reading or listening – of the way parts of a text relate to each other. It has been shown that the ability to see 'wholeness' between parts is a characteristic that only emerges in older children, while forming the gist of longer texts may be difficult before adolescence.

Sociolinguistic ability – being able to adapt our language – depends on a heightened awareness of 'others', which gradually emerges during later childhood, along with the need to identify with a group, which is particularly strong in the teenage years. It also involves being able to use and interpret language according to the context, as well as in non-literal ways, which has been seen to emerge gradually in later childhood and the teenage years. Studies such as Rose (2005) and Bardovi-Harlig and Griffin (2005) suggest, however, that the acquisition of the knowledge associated with sociolinguistic ability in the L2 is heavily dependent on its being taught or demonstrated to the learner.

Strategic ability requires an awareness of both what we, ourselves, and other speakers are achieving in the communication, as well as certain skills such as paraphrasing, and therefore can only be expected to emerge gradually as children mature. Nippold cites 10 years as the age where the child typically shows some awareness of a listener's potential confusion (see Appendix A). It seems reasonable to assume that this would be the case whether communicating in the L1 or the L2.

In short, the age/developmental stage of young learners impacts on the extent to which they are potentially able to acquire all four aspects of CLA. However, the extent to which they actually acquire them and are able to demonstrate them, is affected by the environment in which they are learning.

Domain of Language Use

Having discussed what kind of knowledge or abilities the young learner needs to communicate in an L2, we now consider the use they will put these to: how and in what situations they are expected to use the language, or the domain of language use. Adapted from Weir (1993) this can be described in terms of:

- topics of communication
- purposes of communication
- participants in communication (and how they relate to each other)
- the channel (or media) people communicate through (for example written or spoken, by phone, computer or face-to-face)
- the discourse types/genres of communication.

Each of these aspects of the domain will be covered in turn.

Topics

The *topics* we read, write or talk about, may be seemingly unlimited for a proficient, mature speaker in the L2 but are limited for many, for example, by language proficiency and age, and by what has been focused on in the learning environment.

As a rule, regardless of age, the range of topics covered will begin with what is most familiar, in situations where the language is used or taught, and expand outwards. Age, however, does have an effect on the topics a learner can cope with. The youngest learners are most concerned with themselves, and what they have 'concrete' personal experience of. Older children tend to be more interested in what they do with their age group and relationships with peers. They are gradually more concerned with their views and emotions and have a growing awareness of the society around them and the world beyond. Teenagers are increasingly able to cope with more abstract, complex and often controversial issues.

Individual topics reflecting this development are illustrated in websites such as The British Council's Learn English Kids (http://learnenglish-kids.britishcouncil.org) and Teens (http://learnenglishteens.britishcouncil.org). School curricula can also shed a good deal of light on the topics young learners cover. Rixon's (2013) worldwide survey of English taught as a foreign language in primary schools shows that two-thirds of the 64 countries she investigated specifically listed topics, although the level of precision and detail in these varied. It should be noted, however, that many learners of English, particularly as a second language, i.e. a language used in the particular society, do not follow a plan for English as an L2, but follow a mainstream curriculum for L1 English.

Two quite different school curricula are considered here, one for learners of English taught as a foreign language in Sweden, and one designed for learners of English in an English-speaking context, in the United States.

The Swedish school curriculum for English, current at the time of writing (www.skolverket.se/laroplaner-amnen-och-kurser/grundskoleutbildning/

grundskola/engelska), is roughly summarized in Table 2.1, where the topics shown on the left of the table are gradually added to as the pupils progress through schooling.

Table 2.1: Topics in Current National Curriculum Aims for English as a Foreign Language, Sweden

Grades 1–3 (7–9 years)	Grades 4–6 (10–12 years)	Grades 7–9 (13–16 years)
Topics familiar to the pupils		+ relevant topics
Interests, people and places	+ Everyday situations events and activities	+ how events unfold, relationships and ethical questions
Everyday life in different contexts and in areas where English is used	+ social relationships	+ cultural understanding
	Opinions, feelings and experiences	+ plans for the future

The Curriculum for English as a Second/Additional Language for New Jersey (2012) (http://www.state.nj.us/education/bilingual/curriculum/) is summed up in Table 2.2. Here, the topic areas are more precisely defined and, on the surface, appear quite different from the Swedish aims summarized above.

Table 2.2: Curriculum Aims for English as a Second Language, New Jersey Project, 2012

Grade/age	Topic
Kindergarten (5/6 years)	Creativity, Here We Go, Seasons and Environment, Welcome to the Farm
Grades 1–2 (6–8 years)	Cycles, Families, Seed to Sandwich, Sounds
Grades 3–5 (8–11 years)	Communities, Exploration, Growth and Change, Self-Discovery
Grades 6–8 (11–14 years)	Freedom and Democracy, Holocaust: The Impact of World Conflict on Human Interaction, Probability and Data Analysis, Water is life
Grades 9–12 (14–18 years)	Ecology and Adaptation, Multi-Dimensional Shapes, Shakespearean Drama, The Immigration Experience

However, both curricula reflect a development from concrete and immediate or very familiar topics in earlier childhood, to more abstract societal and expressive topics in the middle years, and finally to more complex, 'distant' and potentially controversial issues. As young learners mature, an increasing experience and knowledge of the world will continually push back the boundaries of what is familiar or understandable, and hence expand the range of topics that can be covered. While specific topics covered by learners in their L2 communication can be assumed to vary considerably, depending on the context, it is reasonable to assume that the nature of the topics as learners mature will follow the broad development illustrated here.

Purposes of Communication

While the purposes of communication in or outside a classroom vary too widely to even attempt any inventory of these, a number of mega-purposes, or functions of language, have been identified, for example by Van Ek and Trim (1993) and Crystal (1997). These typically include:

- giving and seeking information
- expressing and finding out attitudes and feelings
- getting people to do things
- being sociable.

It is worth discussing the extent to which these functions belong to the domain of language use of young learners. There seems no reason to assume that any of them are impossible, at their most basic, even for very young children. However, the ability to perform them skilfully and under a range of circumstances depends on the degree of language ability. This is particularly true of sociolinguistic ability when it comes to getting people to do things, which has been seen to be related to age.

Halliday (2003) cites a number of oral language functions he feels are essential for young children to develop, in order to cope with the early years of schooling. These coincide to some extent with the list above (giving and seeking information and getting people to do things). The functions relating to attitudes and feelings, and being sociable, which are more closely associated with older children and teenagers, have been omitted. Interestingly, Halliday includes the *imaginative* function, which can be expanded to include game playing, story-telling and using language creatively and for fun. In fact, this would not be considered out of place in most progressive secondary school classrooms.

Participants

Younger children are in the process of learning to talk to their peers, which is an important part of their social development. Cekaite (2008) describes the different roles of teachers and peers in interaction in the L2 learning of younger children, with the teachers (ideally) providing more scaffolding to support the learning, while the peers provide opportunities to practise. As children grow older, they are better able to collaborate with others, and from adolescence are better able to see the perspectives of others, including people who they do not know or have much in common with. This can be reflected in their writing as well as their speaking. Teenagers have been found to talk more easily to peers than to adults; in fact, interaction in the L2 has been found to be a complex issue throughout schooling, relating to social factors as well as L2 development (for example, Philp and Duchesne 2008).

Medium (Channel) of Communication

It is taken for granted here that both spoken and written language are firmly in the domain of language use of young learners. But within these (and indeed transcending them), is an ever-growing range of media, used and accessed particularly by young people, who are often more familiar with them than their teachers and parents. The extent to which these are exploited by schools will vary, but few would argue against the assertion that being an L2 user (current and future) should embrace whatever forms of media are used in the L1, in the everyday lives of young people.

Discourse Types/Genres of Communication

The information presented in Chapter 1 and Appendix A on both cognitive/ social and L1 development provides a basis for some conclusions about the discourse types/genres that L2 learners of different ages can cope with. Here, the term 'discourse type' will be used when referring to the spoken language, while 'genre' will be used when referring to the written language.

In the spoken language, the youngest children can take part in conversations with both children and adults, and tell simple stories. Older children can tell interesting and original stories with multiple subplots, mentioning characters' thoughts and feelings. They can negotiate with peers to resolve conflicts, and give clear route directions. Teenagers can produce elaborate and entertaining stories. They can use persuasive strategies, and produce clear arguments and counter arguments. They show a growing ability to solve conflicts through collaboration (Nippold 2006).

In the written language, Nippold concludes that 10 year-olds can write effectively in narrative and descriptive genres, and that persuasive and expository texts emerge after this stage.

These discourse types/genres seem to correspond to the nature of the topics described above as L2 learners progress through primary school and beyond. However, the extent to which learners actually learn and use a range of discourse types and genres remains a cause for concern. Chvala (2012) analysed a series of oral exams in L2 English set by schools for Norwegian 16 year-olds, and found that, while prescribed topics were generally adhered to, the requirement that pupils use a range of discourse type was persistently ignored by the schools. Kibler (2011), addressing the subject of L2 adolescent writers in the US, underlines the need for explicit teaching of genre types. She maintains that a challenge to teachers is using 'students' implicit knowledge of genres, which develops at a very young age' (2011: 213), and building on this to develop formalized rules of genre. She and others, such as Ortmeier-Hooper and Enright (2011), conclude that there is great variation in the degree to which L2 students are given the instruction they need to fulfil their writing potential. What must be concluded is that while the domain of L2 use should include an age-related progression of discourse types/genres such as indicated above, this will not be achieved through maturity alone, and is largely in the hands of educators.

Conclusion

This chapter has covered the subject of communicative language knowledge and ability – what a learner needs to know and do in order to be able to communicate effectively in the L2 – and the domain of language use, defined in terms of what we communicate about, why we do it, who with, and how. The information presented in Chapter 1 on cognitive and social development, and how this is manifested in L1 language use, has been incorporated, backed up by support from a number of findings on L2 language development. Some conclusions have been drawn on how age can affect both the abilities and the domains of use of the language of young learners. The ability to communicate depends not only on a grasp of concepts, from concrete and immediate to distant or abstract, but also on the ability, for example, to link ideas into coherent text in a range of discourse types/genres, and to see the world from the perspectives of others. The domain of use expands in a way which reflects the development in language ability, but is also impacted by the growing knowledge and understanding of the world, as well as by the context of learning. And, as in the case of the L1, what a learner can do in the written language, his/her L2 literacy cannot be taken for granted, and is affected by many factors, the school environment being only one.

Having presented a wide variety of conclusions about the L2 of young learners as they mature, it is now time to bring these together into a system. In the next chapter, we will consider the extent to which the most comprehensive system of this type to date, the CEFR, can be applied to the case of young learners.

3 The Common European Framework of Reference

The previous chapter presented a discussion on how the L2 of young learners is constrained by their age/stage of development, both in terms of their communicative language ability and the domains of their language use. This chapter will build on that discussion, putting the spotlight on the Common European Framework of Reference (CEFR) (Council of Europe 2001), with its associated European Language Portfolio (ELP) (www.coe.int/t/dg4/education/elp/elp-reg/accredited_models/accredited_elp_2010_EN.asp). These instruments describe the ability of language learners as they progress, and provide a yardstick for assessing this ability. Both the CEFR and the ELP have wide currency, within and beyond Europe. This can be exemplified in the case of Taiwan, where the CEFR has been adopted and used as a recognized benchmark, and in Japan, where the CEFRJ has been established, aimed at younger adults, with the lower levels fleshed out.

Moreover, the CEFR is used both for adult learners, for which it was originally intended, and for younger learners, for which it was not. The ELP has been adapted in many forms for younger learners, while CEFR levels are reflected in school curricula, coursebooks and tests. Many sets of 'can-do' statements have been compiled, such as those proposed by Hasselgreen (2003), but the 'official' proficiency levels in the CEFR, such as those presented as *Global descriptors,* remain unadapted for young learners at the time of writing. Therefore, it is considered important to include a discussion here on the extent to which these levels, as they stand, are appropriate to young learners. Little (2006) makes his position on this clear, commenting on the fact that, while the A1 descriptors for spoken interaction could be mastered at any age, C2 descriptors imply heavy cognitive demands which put them well out of the reach of primary or lower secondary school pupils. According to Little:

> This characteristic of the CEFR's levels and scales means that they can be adapted to the needs and circumstances of younger learners to a limited extent only. Those who insist otherwise have usually failed to grasp that a high level of linguistic competence does not necessary entail a precocious range of communicative proficiency (2006: 174).

The question is, are there levels on the scales which can be found to coincide with the developmental stages of learners in different age groups, and if so, do these levels represent the full potential of those younger language learners and users?

The chapter will first briefly introduce the CEFR and ELP, and demonstrate why and in what ways the CEFR is of significance to language teaching and assessment in the case of young learners. It will then seek to establish some tendencies regarding the age/school stage at which certain levels on the CEFR are perceived to be attainable. Levels relating to key aspects of communication will be examined in turn to see if any such perception is justifiable in the light of what has been discussed in Chapters 1 and 2. What emerges should throw light on which levels on the CEFR are potentially within reach of the different age groups. The question will also be put as to whether the CEFR descriptors at these levels fully cover what the young learners in any age group can do, and, if not, where they fall short. Some issues will be discussed which may have to be addressed if the CEFR is ever to be fully suited to use with young learners.

Having focused rather heavily on CEFR levels in this discussion, it is important to add that, as Little and Erickson (2015) point out:

> the CEFR is a great deal more than a collection of proficiency levels and scales... Its action-oriented approach to the description of language proficiency as language use clearly implicates the user-learner's identity and agency, both of which are central to the CEFR's companion piece, the European Language Portfolio (ELP), in which self-assessment plays a key role. Taken together, the CEFR and the ELP imply a rather different assessment culture from one that is often associated with CEFR's reference levels (2015: 122).

The ethos embodied by the CEFR, beyond its levels, will be fundamental to the view of assessment presented in Chapter 4.

The CEFR and the ELP

The CEFR was designed to provide 'a common basis for the elaboration of language syllabuses, curriculum guidelines, examinations, textbooks, etc. across Europe' (Council of Europe 2001: 1). It describes language ability across six levels, A1 to C2, at times with gradation within the levels, in terms of overall proficiency, and what the learner should be able to 'do' within different skills (reading, listening writing, spoken interaction and spoken production). There are also descriptors for basic aspects of the domains of use, such as purpose, topic familiarity, discourse type and participants, with flexibility and adaptation to context on the part of users with respect to domain being encouraged (Council of Europe 2001: xiii). Separate scales for aspects of CLA are included, under the categories of *linguistic competence, sociolinguistic competence* and *pragmatic competence*, which roughly correspond to what was described in Chapter 2 here as *microlinguistic, sociolinguistic* and *textual ability*. Scales are also provided for *interaction strategies*.

The ELP is based on the CEFR, and provides a framework for learners to record and collect evidence of their developing proficiency in any relevant languages. The CEFR levels are most visibly represented through the lists of 'can do' statements within each skill, at a range of levels suitable to the user group for whom the portfolio was designed. As Little (2006: 182) points out, a principal difference between the CEFR and the ELP is that there is no 'canonical' version of the ELP. Member states of the Council of Europe submit their own proposed versions, often for a distinct range of ages, for validation. At the time of writing, there are 127 accredited models of the ELP, of which about 35 are designed for primary school children (approximately aged 6 to 12) with a similar number for secondary school students. Four exist for pre-school learners. This means that more than half of the validated ELPs are for young learners as defined here. This widespread adoption of the ELP, and hence the CEFR, by educators of young learners in Europe, is testimony to the impact these instruments have had. Little (2006) laments the fact that the CEFR has had the greatest impact on testing and assessment, with less impact on the other areas it is intended to be applied to. However, CEFR levels are explicitly referred to in a number of school curricula, for example, in Ireland and Finland, as well as in materials produced for teaching and testing, both by public and private sectors.

Let us consider now the CEFR levels typically cited as objectives for young learners. Rixon's (2013) worldwide survey of primary English language teaching posed the question of what (if any) CEFR level pupils are required to reach at the end of primary school. Most of the 64 countries/ regions surveyed did not have CEFR-related objectives, but 21 did, and responded as follows: A1: 8, A2: 12, B1: 1, B2: 0.

The Irish curriculum for English as a second language, primary and post-primary level, cited in Little (2006), gives descriptors at levels A1, A2 and B1. The Finnish national curricula for basic and higher schooling (http://www.oph.fi/download/47672_core_curricula_basic_education_3. pdf and http://www.oph.fi/english/curricula_and_qualifications/general_ upper_secondary_education) cover foreign languages in addition to 'native languages' for children who are bilingual in the two official languages (Finnish and Swedish). CEFR levels are split into three bands at A1 level and two at other levels. At 6th grade (aged 12/13 years), A2.1 is cited as the highest objective (in comprehension) for English as a first foreign language (FL1), and B1.2 for the native languages. For 9th grade, the corresponding levels are B1.1 (English FL1) and B2.1 (native languages). At upper secondary level, the objective for English FL1 is B2.1. It is interesting to note the levels defined for native languages, as this provides an insight into what is regarded as cognitively within reach of learners at these stages.

ELPs and tests for primary school children show similar limitations to levels in the range A1 to B1. This is exemplified by the CILT National Centre for Languages Junior portfolio (www.primarylanguages.org.uk/res ources/assessment_and_recording/european_languages_portfolio.aspx) and the Norwegian primary school portfolio, *Språkperm 6–12*. The Norwegian secondary school portfolio, *Språkperm 12–18*, offers 'can dos' as high as C2 (www.fremmedspraksenteret.no/nor/fremmedspraksenteret/larings-ressurser/den-europeiske-sprakpermen). In their tests of young learners, Cambridge English Language Assessment offer tests for children up to about 12 years at levels A1 and A2 (https://www.teachers.cambridgeesol.org/ts/exams/younglearnersandforschools).

While it is not feasible to carry out a comprehensive survey of all ELPs and curricula, many of these being accessible only in the national language(s), it seems there is a tendency for primary school children to be considered to have a 'ceiling' on the CEFR of around A2 to B1. For secondary school students, it is more difficult to identify such a ceiling, as this may be dependent on contextual factors, such as whether lower and upper secondary school are treated as an entity.

Analysing CEFR Levels with Respect to Age

A closer inspection of CEFR levels on salient descriptor scales is undertaken here, in order to shed some light on whether the demands made of learners at particular levels put them beyond the reach of young learners at different developmental stages. Accepting Little's (2006) assertion that A1 descriptors (of spoken interaction) are reachable even by very young children, the focus here will be on levels A2 and above, bearing in mind that young learners are defined here as younger children (about 5/6 to 8/9 years), older children (about 8/9 to 12/13 years) and teenagers (about 13 to 17 years).

We will look at selected descriptors for each level from A2 to C1, in order to identify, on the basis of what has been revealed in Chapters 1 and 2, the lowest age group which appears to be able to meet most of the requirements of each level. We take for granted that what learners in any age group can do will be doable by all age groups above that. It is essential to bear in mind that no claim is made that all learners in the age group will be able to reach the particular level in an L2. The point is that they are not barred from reaching the level by age/development alone. It should be added that the descriptors should be regarded as referring to 'ordinary' language use, and not specifically to test items. A child's ability to 'take the initiative' in conversation, for example, may be straightforward with a friend, but more challenging with an oral examiner.

For A2, the *global descriptor* is:

> Can understand sentences and frequently used expressions related to areas of most immediate relevance (for example very basic personal and family information, shopping, local geography, employment). Can communicate in simple and routine tasks requiring a simple and direct exchange of information on familiar and routine matters. Can describe in simple terms aspects of his/her background, immediate environment and matters in areas of immediate need (Council of Europe 2001: 24).

Leaving aside the fact that the actual themes and situations of communication suggested here may not apply to young learners, the characteristics presented, in terms of the immediacy of topics, the routine nature of tasks, and the functions performed, are all compatible with what has been described in the previous chapters as within the domains of use of younger children, in the early years of schooling. What is described in the CEFR *self-assessment grid* for the specific skills (Council of Europe 2001: 26) shows that no more than very simple language is required at A2, although reading and writing clearly require literacy skills beyond those of some of the youngest children.

The description of *general linguistic ability* for A2 state:

> Can produce brief everyday expressions in order to satisfy simple needs of a concrete type: personal details, daily routines, wants and needs, requests for information. Can use basic sentence patterns and communicate with memorised phrases, groups of a few words and formulae about themselves and other people, what they do, places, possessions etc. Has a limited repertoire of short memorised phrases covering predictable survival situations; frequent breakdowns and misunderstandings occur in non-routine situations (Council of Europe 2001: 110).

This description also reflects the limited, familiar and 'concrete' nature of the lexicon and the low demands on syntax, which have been demonstrated here to be within the reach of younger children.

The scale of *sociolinguistic appropriateness*, even at 'higher' A2, states:

> Can perform and respond to basic language functions, such as
> information exchange and requests, and express opinions and atti-
> tudes in a simple way. Can socialise simply but effectively using
> the simplest common expressions and following basic routines
> (Council of Europe 2001: 122).

This description does not imply the need for a well-developed awareness
of others, nor the ability to make appropriate language choices, so, again,
should be within the reach of most younger children.

The discourse competences cited for A2 include:

> Can use simple techniques to start, maintain, or end a short con-
> versation. Can initiate, maintain and close simple, face-to-face
> conversation. Can tell a story or describe something in a simple
> list of points. Can use the most frequently occurring connectors to
> link simple sentences in order to tell a story or describe something
> as a simple list of points (Council of Europe 2001: 124–25).

This reflects what has been presented here about the genre/discourse types
typically used by younger children, as well as their level of syntactic
attainment.

In short, it can be concluded that, provided topics and situations are
adapted to their environment, young children in the early school years, up
to roughly 8/9 years, can reasonably be expected to have the *potential* to
reach level A2 in an L2, although may not have the literacy skills necessary to carry out the reading and writing normally required at A2. To put it
another way, young learners in all the age groups defined here should have
the potential to reach level A2.

For B1, the *global scale* states:

> Can understand the main points of clear standard input on familiar
> matters regularly encountered in work, school, leisure, etc. Can
> deal with most situations likely to arise whilst travelling in an area
> where the language is spoken. Can produce simple connected text
> on topics which are familiar or of personal interest. Can describe
> experiences and events, dreams, hopes and ambitions and briefly
> give reasons and explanations for opinions and plans (Council of
> Europe 2001: 24).

Here, the topics extend beyond the immediate and highly personal, with
'familiar' being a key term, thus reflecting what was associated with older
children in the discussion on domain in Chapter 2. The nature of what can
be described or explained ventures into the abstract, although not requiring

particular insight into the perspectives of others, and is compatible with what has been discussed here relating to the cognitive and social development of older children as they approach adolescence. This is also the case for what is described in the *self-assessment grid* (Council of Europe 2001: 26), on the different skills, which includes the expression of feelings and reactions, for example, to a book or film, yet staying within the area of what is familiar to the learner.

While in some respects, for example, producing simple connected texts on familiar topics, the above descriptor would not exclude younger children, there are several elements, notably in the types of discourse referred to (*describing dreams, hopes and ambitions, and briefly giving reasons and explanations for opinions and plans*) which seems to put this descriptor beyond the reach of many younger children.

The description of *general linguistic ability* for lower B1 states:

> Has enough language to get by, with sufficient vocabulary to express him/herself with some hesitation and circumlocutions on topics such as family, hobbies and interests, work, travel, and current events, but lexical limitations cause repetition and even difficulty with formulation at times (Council of Europe 2001: 110).

For upper B1, the corresponding statement is:

> Has a sufficient range of language to describe unpredictable situations, explain the main points in an idea or problem with reasonable precision and express thoughts on abstract or cultural topics such as music and films (Council of Europe 2001: 110).

'Getting by' on familiar topics, as summed up in the descriptor for lower B1, should be within the reach of most older children, and even many younger ones. However, in the descriptor for upper B1, the specific reference to abstract or cultural topics, as well as to the abilities to identify main points and to give explanations with some precision all concur with what was shown, in the previous chapters, to emerge only as children approach adolescence. This suggests that these criteria may only fully be in the reach of older children at the highest end of the age range, and that lower B1 may be a more realistic attainable level for many children in this age group.

On the scale of *sociolinguistic appropriateness*, the descriptor for B1 states:

> Can perform and respond to a wide range of language functions, using their most common exponents in a neutral register. Is aware of the salient politeness conventions and acts appropriately. Is aware of, and looks out for signs of, the most significant

differences between the customs, usages, attitudes, values and
beliefs prevalent in the community concerned and those of his or
her own (Council of Europe 2001: 122).

This suggests some roughly-tuned awareness of others, and a desire to
cooperate and 'fit in', characteristics which have been seen to emerge in
older children. Younger children are not only less socially tuned-in, but
more readily take direction from those around them, and are unlikely to
make independent language choices required to bring about sociolinguistic
appropriateness.

Discourse competences for B1 include:

Can initiate, maintain and close simple face-to-face conversation
on topics that are familiar or of personal interest. Can reasonably
fluently relate a straightforward narrative or description as a linear
sequence of points. Can link a series of shorter, discrete simple
elements into a connected, linear sequence of points (Council of
Europe 2001: 125).

These competences require a grasp of the basic skills of syntax and conversation, as well as the ability to tell stories. While these skills are refined
in older childhood and adolescence, in its most basic interpretation, this
descriptor could be regarded as within the reach even of younger children.

Thus, while there are a small number of elements in the descriptions of
level B1 which are within the reach of younger children, and other elements
which may be at the very limit of what pre-adolescent children can do, the
overall conclusion must be that the lowest age group for whom level B1 is
generally reachable is that of older children. Interestingly, level B1.2 was
given as the objective in the Finnish curriculum for native language (bilingual) speakers of 12/13 years, which reflects the perception of upper B1 as
a 'ceiling' for this age group.

For B2, the *global scale* states:

Can understand the main ideas of complex texts on both concrete
and abstract topics, including technical discussions in his/her field
of specialisation. Can interact with a degree of fluency and spon-
taneity that makes regular interaction with native speakers quite
possible without strain for either party. Can produce clear, detailed
text on a wide range of subjects and explain a viewpoint on a
topical issue giving the advantages and disadvantages of various
options (Council of Europe 2001: 24).

The wide range and the complex nature of topics suggested here is similar
to what was presented in Chapter 2 on the discussion of topics for teenagers.

Moreover, the ability to not only see other perspectives on an issue, but to argue for and against, has been shown here to be a feature of post-adolescent development.

This is further expanded in the *self-assessment grid* (Council of Europe 2001: 27), which puts considerable demands on the learner, in terms of world knowledge and genre knowledge, as well the ability to understand the attitude or viewpoint of writers. These attributes are all shown to be acquired during the teenage years and beyond.

The description of *general linguistic ability* for B2 states:

> Can express him/herself clearly and without much sign of having to restrict what he/she wants to say. Has a sufficient range of language to be able to give clear descriptions, express viewpoints and develop arguments without much conspicuous searching for words, using some complex sentence forms to do so (Council of Europe 2001: 110).

Besides an extensive vocabulary, this clearly requires a quite high degree of syntactic attainment, which has been shown to develop significantly during the teenage years, and into adulthood.

On the scale of *sociolinguistic appropriateness*, the descriptor for B2 states:

> Can express him or herself confidently, clearly and politely in a formal or informal register, appropriate to the situation and person(s) concerned. Can with some effort keep up with and contribute to group discussions even when speech is fast and colloquial. Can sustain relationships with native speakers without unintentionally amusing or irritating them or requiring them to behave other than they would with a native speaker. Can express him or herself appropriately in situations and avoid crass errors of formulation (Council of Europe 2001: 122).

This requires considerable social skills on the part of the speaker, which may only be developed with the support of the learning environment, and may never be reached, even as an adult. It is at least beyond what could reasonably be asked of most children below the teenage years.

Discourse competences for B2 include:

> Can initiate, maintain and end discourse appropriately with effective turn-taking. Can initiate discourse, take his/her turn when appropriate and end conversation when he/she needs to, though he/she may not always do this elegantly. Can use stock phrases (for example "That's a difficult question to answer") to gain time and

keep the turn whilst formulating what to say. Can use a variety of linking words efficiently to mark clearly the relationships between ideas. Can develop a clear description or narrative, expanding and supporting his/her main points with relevant supporting detail and examples. Can use a limited number of cohesive devices to link his/her utterances into clear, coherent discourse, though there may be some "jumpiness" in a long contribution (Council of Europe 2001: 125–26).

The ability to tell a complex and interesting story has been shown to be a feature of the teenage years. Using a range of linking words and cohesive devices has been shown to develop particularly after adolescence.

Thus, it would appear that B2 is a level which seems unlikely to be reached before adolescence, but is potentially within the grasp of teenagers as they mature. Again, this is reflected in the Finnish curriculum aims for native language speakers, where B2.1 is the objective for 16 year-olds.

For C1, the *global scale* states:

Can understand a wide range of demanding, longer texts, and recognise implicit meaning. Can express him/herself fluently and spontaneously without much obvious searching for expressions. Can use language flexibly and effectively for social, academic and professional purposes. Can produce clear, well-structured, detailed text on complex subjects, showing controlled use of organisational patterns, connectors and cohesive devices (Council of Europe 2001: 24).

The *self-assessment grid* descriptors (Council of Europe 2001: 27) include:

I can understand long and complex factual and literary texts, appreciating distinctions of style (reading).

and

I can use language flexibly and effectively for social and professional purposes. I can formulate ideas and opinions with precision and relate my contribution skilfully to those of other speakers (speaking).

Without exploring this level further, it is possible to draw some conclusions on what is demanded at C1. Firstly, it has been shown in Chapter 1 and specified in Appendix A, that the knowledge and skills demanded at this level continue to develop in young adulthood; these include an expanding vocabulary, the advanced use of conjunctions and adverbial conjuncts, and the skilful use of argumentative strategies. Moreover, unlike the levels examined so far, the descriptors for C1 do not seem to represent a level to which everyone would naturally progress, even in their L1. To reach this level would normally require a high degree of education, or considerable experience with a range of discourse types. It is worth noting that in the Finnish national matriculation exam (for students at the top extreme of our teenage group) for English as the first foreign language, about 5 to10% of students are assessed as 'beyond B2.2', or occasionally as C1.1 (personal correspondence with Sauli Takala, 2014).

Thus, this level is perhaps best regarded as one which *may* be within the reach of a number of learners at the upper limit of the age range for young learners, building further on the skills and knowledge described for B2, which has been argued here to be generally unreachable before the teenage years.

Conclusion

The findings from this brief analysis of descriptors at a range of CEFR levels, in the light of factors of development discussed in the previous chapters, are summed up in Table 3.1, which shows a correspondence between age groups and the CEFR levels potentially attainable (i.e. on the basis of maturity). It demonstrates the levels which we perceive to be reachable by the different age groups. It should be noted that the correlation between CEFR levels and age is not totally clear-cut. There will always be occasional elements within the levels that may not pose a problem for learners younger than the ages shown.

Table 3.1: Correspondence Between Age Groups and CEFR Levels Potentially Attainable

Age groups	Limits of CEFR levels potentially attainable
Young children (roughly between 5/6 years and 8/9 years)	A2 Reading and writing levels will depend on the emergence of literacy
Older children (roughly between 8/9 years and 12/13 years)	B1
Teenagers (roughly between 13 and 17 years)	B2
Exceptional older teenagers	C1

It is also worth emphasizing that the age ranges given here are deliberately open and approximate, as there are huge individual and even cultural differences in the rates of cognitive development. The above correspondence takes 'normal' literacy development (as described in Chapter 1) for granted. When this is not the case, the CEFR level attainable, not only in written language proficiency, but also, to some degree, in spoken, will be affected.

Some questions remain unanswered by what has emerged here, and touch on some shortcomings of the CEFR, with respect to its application to young learners. The first concerns whether the levels themselves, as they are defined, can be regarded as the ultimate potential achievement of the learner group involved. In other words, can a child of say, 7 years, do no more than what is described in the scales for A2? Can an 11year-old progress no further than B1? The descriptors at these levels imply limitations in the range of linguistic knowledge which may well not apply to individual young learners. Regardless of the school curricula objectives, some children, for example, through home languages, will have near-native proficiency. And it is well-documented that children pick up language outside school, as exemplified by Lefever's (2012) study of Icelandic children, many of whom are found to have a wide repertoire of English before even starting to learn this in school. There appears to be no clear way of describing the CEFR level, for instance, of a child too young to fully reach B2, yet clearly advancing beyond B1.

A second question regards the gradation of the CEFR scale. It has been demonstrated here that it may take several years to advance from one level to the next, which makes the CEFR as it stands too rough an instrument to show progress in a way that is useful or motivating to the young learner. It is also worth noting that, as has been shown here, there are some elements of levels (for example discourse competence at B1) which may be reachable before others, and that the descriptors themselves, at times, show quite distinct lower and upper levels. The Finnish curriculum exemplifies a way of overcoming this by dividing each level into two (three in the case of A1). These levels are presented in some details in the Appendix to the Finnish national curriculum for Upper Secondary school (www.oph.fi/english/curricula_and_qualifications/general_upper_secondary_education) up to level C1.1. This method is also used by Hasselgreen, Kaledaite, Maldonado Martin, and Pizorn (2011) in the European Centre for Modern Language's Assessment of Young Learner Literacy (AYLLIT) project, whereby a scale for assessing the writing of upper primary school learners was developed, with in-between levels, such as A1/A2, described in detail (see Appendix B.1). Incidentally, this scale begins with the level 'approaching A1', and finishes at 'above B1'. While the official CEFR descriptors at times are split into upper and lower degrees of a level, this is not done generally, and lays the scales open to rather ad hoc representations of split levels by individual users.

Finally, an important question must be raised: Are individual levels the same for different age groups? For instance, is the language ability of a 12 year-old at B1 the same as that of a 16 year-old at B1? A key factor which can affect language performance at B1 is the use of the term 'familiar'. What is familiar to a 16 year-old encompasses far more than when that person was 12. A growing world-knowledge and an expanding range of experience, as well as an understanding of more abstract and complex ideas, will affect what the older learner will be able to produce and understand, even if the proficiency level can still be described as B1. This has been the subject of studies such as Helness (2012), which investigated the written language vocabulary of groups of learners aged 12/13 years and 15/16 years, both having been rated as being at similar levels on the CEFR. The comparison was fraught with complicating factors, not the least of which was the fact that the tasks given reflected the ages of the learners, and thus 'muddied' the picture in terms of the kind of language they produced. Clearly, if we are to rate different age groups using the same scale, this is a question that must be taken seriously, and it requires more input from research.

The analysis in this chapter is based on general CEFR descriptors that are not specific to any skill such as reading and writing. It has provided us with a way of judging what is a reasonable overall level to regard as a maximum, potential objective for young learners in the different age groups. In the chapters on assessing particular skills, these levels will be used as a rough guide to what can be expected at the various stages.

Having explored the L2 of young learners with respect to what they can potentially do with their language across a range of ages, we are now in a position to begin investigating how this might be assessed. This will be the subject of the remainder of the book, with a general introduction to the topic in the next chapter.

4   Assessing the L2 of Young Learners

The discussion so far has been of a generally tangible nature – relating to the likely linguistic capacity of young learners, the particular competences they require to communicate in an L2 and under what conditions of use, and how the levels on the CEFR appear to be reachable as learners mature. In this chapter, language itself will take a back seat, while the spotlight will be put on issues and principles of language assessment.

As the following chapters will specifically relate to language testing, the focus in this chapter will gradually shift from a broader view of assessment to testing. However, it must be emphasized that the meaning of 'testing' here is not confined to formal or summative testing. As will be made clear below, testing is an essential component in informal and formative assessment. And many of the principles associated with good testing hold good for a wide range of 'non-testing' assessment practices.

The EALTA guidelines for good practice in language testing and assessment (www.ealta.eu.org/guidelines.htm) state: 'a number of general principles apply: respect for the students/examinees, responsibility, fairness, reliability, validity and collaboration among the parties involved'. Little and Erickson (2015: 127), referring to these guidelines and their underlying concepts, state:

When planning, analysing and evaluating any type of assessment, it is necessary to answer five questions, with these principles and concepts in mind:

- Why is the assessment being undertaken?
- What is being assessed, what is the construct?
- How is it being evaluated, and fed back or reported?
- Who are the agents in the assessment process?
- What are the intended and envisaged uses and consequences of the assessment?

The principles and issues associated with these questions will form the basis of this chapter, and will be reflected in those that follow. The first question, concerning the purpose of the assessment, will be dealt with at the outset, being fundamental to the structuring of this chapter.

Assessment can have many purposes, such as diagnostic, placement, certifying, or simply to find out if pupils have learnt what has been covered in class on a particular day. Two overarching purposes are frequently cited: *formative*, in support of learning, or *summative*, for reporting progress or performance (Harlen and Gardner 2010: 27).

Formative assessment is increasingly acknowledged to be an essential and integral part of the learning process throughout schooling, from kindergarten upwards, for example as described in Clarke (2008). Summative assessment, on the other hand, is perhaps most closely associated with secondary schooling, where both internal and external examining tend to be systematically carried out. However, summative assessment is not entirely the preserve of the secondary sector. In Rixon's (2013) worldwide survey of primary English language teaching, 34 of the 64 countries/regions responded that children are required to be formally assessed at the end of primary school, 22 by external tests or exams and 12 using internally designed means of assessment. Although the consequences of this assessment differed from country to country, the general purpose of the assessment can be regarded as summative, rather than formative.

It is tempting to make a direct association between classroom/teacher assessment and formative assessment on one hand, and summative assessment and testing on the other. However, Harlen and Gardner (2010: 27) state:

> Teacher assessment comprises a large collection of information gleaned from the daily classroom interactions between pupils and teachers, and between pupils and pupils. The interactions cover many different types of process including the dynamic assessments of questioning and feedback, the reflective assessments of self- and peer-assessment, the sharing of learning goals and the criteria that indicate their achievement, and the long-term progression-related evidence from pupils' work. Such a wealth of evidence is primarily used in an ad hoc support of learning 'in the moment' (assessments for formative purposes) but can also be captured in suitable forms for reporting progress and performance (assessments for summative judgements).

Thus, classroom/teacher assessment can, at times, be used for summative purposes. It is also the case that test results can be included in the 'evidence' of learning which is primarily used for formative purposes. In the discussion in this chapter, however, testing and formative assessment will be treated separately. Features of formative assessment will be discussed first, focusing on what makes any assessment formative, or integral to the learning process. Principles of language testing – which is not regarded here as either inherently formative or summative – will then be presented. Again, it must be emphasized that many of these testing principles apply to forms of assessment which do not involve testing, such as classroom interaction.

Features of Formative Assessment

Five distinguishing features of formative assessment are cited by Wiliam (2011: 46). These features are reflected widely in what is acknowledged to constitute good formative assessment, (for example, in Clarke 2008: 11 and Harlen and Gardner 2010: 48).

1. Engineering effective classroom discussions, activities and learning tasks that elicit evidence of learning
2. Clarifying, sharing and understanding learning intentions and criteria for success
3. Providing feedback that moves learning forward
4. Activating learners as owners of their own learning
5. Activating learners as instructional resources for one another.

Engineering effective classroom discussions, activities and learning tasks that elicit evidence of learning

Activities which elicit this evidence come in a wide range of forms, including tests, homework tasks, reading aloud and story writing. Validity is a highly salient issue to this evidence gathering, but the discussion on this will be left to the next section on language testing. Classroom interaction is arguably the most central means of eliciting evidence of learning. In their investigation into formative assessment of younger primary school children in the UK, Torrance and Pryor (1998) concluded that, while there was a general perception among teachers and policymakers that classroom interaction was fairly straightforward and intuitive and that questions could be asked clearly to find out what children knew, this was not actually the case. In a study of classroom interaction in classes as part of the National Literacy Strategy in primary school classrooms in the UK, Smith, Hardman, Wall and Mroz (2004) came to similar conclusions about the ineffectiveness of much of the interaction. On the basis of both of these studies, a number of characteristics of good classroom interaction can be identified, including the avoidance of ritualistic, highly structured exchange patterns and, as far as possible, asking open and genuine questions, enabling pupils to do most of the talking and show what they know.

Clarifying, Sharing and Understanding Learning Intentions and Criteria for Success

While it is not always wise to begin every lesson by presenting the learning aim (Wiliam 2011; Clarke 2001), there would be few who would argue against the value of young learners being aware of where they are heading in their learning and how success will be judged. Clarke (2001: 25) gives the following steps for developing a 'learning culture' in the primary school classroom.

- Clarify learning intentions at planning stage.
- Make it an expectation for children.
- Explain the learning intention, in 'child-speak' if necessary.
- Invite children to say how they know this has been done [the criteria for success].
- Write the success criterion or criteria.
- The 'aside': say *why* this is an important thing to learn – the 'big picture'.
- Get the children to read out the learning intention and criteria.

In the case of language learning, the ELP, or adapted CEFR scales, illustrate the way learners can be helped to understand the overall intention of their learning in individual skills, and to set personal goals. Cameron (2001: 236) maintains that 'children of 7 and 8 years of age can begin to understand criteria for good performance, and if these are simply phrased may be able to use the foreign language'. Examples of this can be seen in the CILT junior ELP (http://www.agtv.vic.edu.au/files/Website%202015/8871-junior-passport.pdf). Wiliam (2011) suggests many ways of involving learners at all school stages in the setting of criteria, such as their selecting a piece of language production which they judge to be good, and trying to work out why they think it was good.

Providing Feedback that Moves Learning Forward

Stobart (2006: 141) characterizes good feedback in formative assessment as follows.

- It is clearly linked to the learning intention.
- The learner understands the success criteria/standard.
- It gives cues at appropriate levels on how to bridge the gap [between what the pupil can do and what is aimed for]:

- o self-regulatory/metacognitive
- o process/deep learning
- o task/surface learning.
- It focuses on the task rather than the learner (self/ego).
- It challenges, requires action, and is achievable.

Two of these points warrant further explanation. Giving cues at appropriate levels of feedback can be illustrated as follows. Self-regulatory/metacognitive feedback gives advice to the pupil on how to help him/herself to acquire the particular skill or knowledge involved, for example ways of memorizing vocabulary. Process/deep learning feedback helps the pupil to understand underlying concepts or patterns, such as how to form plurals of nouns. And task/surface learning applies to feedback which is specific to the particular item, such as a wrongly-used word.

Focusing feedback on the task rather than the learner encourages *learning goals*, where the principal aim is to learn. Learner-focused feedback, giving praise or rewards, may encourage pupils to have *performance goals*, where their principal aim is to be judged favourably, or seen to do well. Clarke (2008) highlights the danger to younger children, who generally start off with learning goals, of the overuse of rewards such as stars and smiley faces, which lead them to develop performance goals. The overuse of grading, rather than task-related comments, at higher school levels can have a similar effect as is illustrated by Wiliam (2011).

An example of task-based feedback on children's writing can be seen in the AYLLIT (Assessment of Young Learner LITeracy) project material (Hasselgreen, Kaledaite, Maldonado Martin, and Pizorn 2011: 27–31) (see also www.ecml.at/tabid/277/PublicationID/63/Default.aspx). A piece of writing is presented, which has been assessed using the AYLLIT scale of descriptors (see Appendix B.1). The section of the descriptor scale appropriate to the individual's level of the writing is used, and kept as a record for the child; the teacher is advised to write a short comment below the scale, based on the categories in the scale, indicating what is good and less good, where the pupil has made progress and what can usefully be worked on. An example of corrective feedback is shown (2011: 30), whereby the child is given the opportunity to work on two problem areas: the past tense of verbs and some miscellaneous spelling errors. A brief explanation of the grammar is given and the child is required to find the past tense of a group of verbs, then to correct those in his/her text. The words which were misspelt are presented for the child to copy, then to correct in the text. This corrective feedback is essentially at two levels – process/deep learning and task/surface learning. Moreover, the requirement to find out past tense forms of verbs, and to correct the text, can be regarded as feedback at the self-regulatory/ metacognitive level.

Activating Learners as Owners of Their Own Learning, and As Instructional Resources for One Another

This feature of formative assessment involves 'agency' in learning and assessment. If assessment is to feed back into learning, clearly the learner has to take some role as agent in the assessment process, either by actively responding to assessment and feedback from others, or by actively reflecting on his/her own performance and learning processes, and taking responsibility for adjusting these. The notion that self-assessment and self-learning go hand-in-hand lies at the heart of the CEFR/ELP. Little (2012: 277) states that 'the ELP supports the operationalization of three principles that…are fundamental to the development of language learner autonomy: learner involvement, learner reflection and reflective as well as communicative target language use'. Little goes on to say:

> The three parts of the ELP play different though complementary roles in a classroom dynamic calculated to foster the development of learner autonomy. The language passport provides a focus for periodic stock-taking; the dossier gathers together work in progress from which learners periodically select samples that demonstrate their learning achievement; and mediating between passport and dossier, the language biography stimulates and supports the processes on which reflective learning depends. Learner self-assessment lies at the centre of these processes. It is clearly relevant at the end of each phase of learning, when learners must decide whether or not they have achieved their goals. But it is equally relevant to goal setting, whose effectiveness depends on a firm understanding of what has already been learnt, and to monitoring, which is a matter of assessing interim progress in relation to whatever goals have been set (Little 2012: 227).

The CILT junior portfolio (see CILT website) gives a basis not only for children to assess what they 'can do', for example in 'talking to someone', but also to consider how they learn languages, with prompts and suggestions for:

- things I like doing
- things I am good at
- things I find difficult
- I learn best when…

While the youngest children may not be able to judge their performance in any absolute way, as was maintained in Chapter 1, they are able to say whether they like doing something, and roughly what they have learnt (Cameron 2001: 236). Cameron goes on to suggest that peer assessment can be a good halfway stage to self-assessment, for example with the children exchanging pieces of their writing, and saying what they think is good, and what can make it better. Clarke (2001: 45) suggests using a poster in the classroom with some fundamental questions for children to consider after doing a piece of work, such as:

- what really made you think/did you find difficult while you were learning to…?
- what helped you (for example a friend, the teacher, new equipment, a book, your own thinking) when something got tricky about learning to…?
- what do you need more help with about learning to…?
- what are you most pleased with about learning to…?
- what have you learnt that is new about learning to…?

(Adapted from Clarke 2001: 41)

Older children and teenagers can benefit from using self-assessment checklists from time to time in the language class, for example to be handed in with a piece a piece of writing, checking for points such as:

- I did the task fully
- I used words that were suitable for the theme
- I used a range of 'connectors' between sentences
- I used paragraphs appropriately
- I made sure there was a logical flow in the writing
- I checked my grammar 'endings'
- I checked my spellings.

Using such a list can share the responsibility for assessing the writing between the pupil and teacher, as well as raising the pupil's awareness of criteria for good writing at a particular level/school stage.

Dynamic Assessment

Before moving on to issues most associated with language testing, it is worth giving some attention to the concept of Dynamic Assessment (DA), which is an approach based on Vygotsky's (1978) Zone of Proximal Development, offering the teacher a chance to assess what is potentially within the learner's reach, rather than what s/he is able to use independently. Lantolf and Poehner (2010) discuss DA as part of L2 language classroom practice, emphasizing that DA is not a uniform methodology in itself, but rather an approach based on the conviction that 'independent performance is insufficient to fully understand abilities and that important insights into development are gained when mediation is offered as performance begins to break down' (2010: 15). They use the terms 'interventionist' and 'interactionist' to denote two distinct conceptualizations of DA. The former approach involves various types of mediation, including questions and cues, following a strict progression from implicit to explicit, until a resolution is reached. Interactionist DA 'places no such restrictions on mediation but instead demands that the mediator do everything possible to help the learner stretch beyond his/her current independent performance, short of giving the answer, although even this might promote development if it occurs at a propitious point in the interaction' (2010: 15). The advantage of the latter approach seems to be in its impact on development in the learner, while the former approach allows for easier and more precise detection of difficulties by the mediator.

Principles of Language Testing

Much has been written on the principles of language testing (see, for example, Davies 1990 and Bachmann and Palmer 1996). At its most basic, a common understanding of what characterizes a good test includes the following: it has a clear *purpose* (there is a shared understanding of why the test is given); it is *valid* (it tests what it is supposed to and serves the purpose for which it is intended); it is *reliable* (the results are accurate and not subject to random factors); it is *fair* (no individual or group is disadvantaged); it has good *washback* effect (the test influences what is taught/learnt in a positive way); and it is *practical* to carry out. The EALTA Guidelines for Good Practice (www.ealta.eu.org/guidelines.htm) emphasize the need for *transparency*; information on the test, including the *criteria for assessment*, should be shared with all concerned, especially those taking it. They also highlight the *consequences* of the testing, including *feedback* to students.

A full discussion of these characteristics is beyond the scope of this book, but a number of them will be commented on from the perspective of the testing of young learners. Some additional issues will be discussed: degree of *support* given, as well as the '*doability*' and *interest* level of the tasks. Clearly there is a degree of overlap between these principles and what was presented in the previous section on formative assessment, and those issues already discussed will not be addressed in any depth here.

The first point to make is that all of the above characteristics are as relevant to young learners as to adults. A case can also be made for applying them equally to informal classroom testing as to formal examining, although the balance between them, as well as what is done to ensure them, may be rather different. To achieve reliability in a national exam, for example, extensive piloting and sampling is required, which in a classroom test would not be not feasible, although it is advisable to 'try out' items before using them. Rating of written or spoken performance in high-stakes testing is normally carried out by multiple raters, trained to use the scoring system; in classroom testing this is not the case, but the consistent use of a transparent rating scale will enhance the reliability of any scoring that may be used. It is worth noting that Wiliam (2011) argues the case for ensuring reliability even in assessment through classroom dialogue; a teacher questioning his/her class to find out how well they have understood something should not rely on a handful of eager respondents, but sample widely, preferably using techniques to include the whole class.

Validity in testing can encompass many aspects, including the test's washback and how its results are used, which Bachmann and Palmer (1996) refer to as a test's 'impact'. The notion of validity has evolved from a focus on 'what' is tested, to include 'how' and 'why' a test is given, as well as how the result is interpreted and acted upon; it has also expanded to include non-testing forms of assessment (Moss, Girard and Haniford 2006). At its core, validity can be regarded as the extent to which an assessment gathers evidence of the construct, or underlying abilities and knowledge it is supposed to be assessing, as well as the extent to which it does not measure other things. Messick (1996: 257) refers to the violation of these as 'construct underrepresentation' and 'construct irrelevant variance' respectively. If we are assessing learners' communicative language ability, it is most natural to use communicative tasks, sampling widely from the appropriate domain of use and allowing learners to show their full range of abilities (for example, textual and sociolinguistic), to ensure the construct is not underrepresented. If we are assessing a particular skill, such as listening, we should avoid too much reading, which is irrelevant in this case. In the case of young learners, there are many aspects of tasks which may affect their performance and lead to construct irrelevant variance; this will be returned to later in this chapter.

Moss Girard and Haniford (2006) emphasize the role in validity of *interpretations, decisions* and *actions* (IDAs) based on the evidence arising from an assessment, whether this is testing of a more formal nature, or classroom assessment of any form. Many factors, including the assessment activity itself, or the social context, can affect the outcome, and a teacher should ideally draw on evidence from different assessment 'events' to ensure a reasonable interpretation of what the evidence indicates about the learner's ability or knowledge. Deciding what to do as a result of this and acting upon it can involve such considerations as the characteristics of the learner(s); it can also give the teacher the opportunity to reflect on and adjust his/her own practices and, hopefully, the resources at his/her disposal.

Regarding the *purpose* of testing, it is particularly important that any testing of young learners is justified, and that both the tester and test-taker understand what this purpose is. McKay (2005) emphasizes the vulnerability of younger learners, and the potentially devastating effect of failure; a fear of testing can take root at a very young age. The first lesson to take from this is that testing should not be done for testing's sake. Nor can it be taken for granted that younger learners always understand what the teacher is trying to find out. Cameron (2001: 21) cites the fact that children often want to please the teacher and so pretend that they understand something. Teachers themselves should have clarity as to which underlying skill(s) they want to test and should let the pupils know this, as well as how the assessment will help them in the long run.

Also associated with the vulnerability of children is the aspect of '*doability*' of test tasks. It is important that children feel that they are able to succeed, to some extent at least. McKay (2005: 15) stresses the need to include some tasks that virtually all children can manage, which applies to all tests, from informal classroom ones to national tests. Ideally, easy tasks should come first, with a progression in the degree of difficulty, or even built-in choices or 'opting out' points. Children may become demotivated and simply give up when a task is too difficult. Also affecting the doability of tasks is the familiarity of the format or other aspects of the items. This can be achieved in a classroom test by sticking to task types that pupils have used in learning (Cameron 2001: 226), and in externally designed tests by providing practice tasks.

A further factor to consider is the degree of *support* that learners are given. From a Vygotskyan perspective, it can be argued, as Cameron (2001: 219) does, that we can only truly assess what children know, or are capable of, when we allow them to show this in interaction, for example with the teacher. This incorporates what was characterized above as *Dynamic Assessment*. While such support is not always possible in a test situation, it can be borne in mind when interpreting results. If a child gets a test result which causes concern, the teacher should try to go through some tasks with the child after the testing, to see where the problem(s) are, and to ascertain what the child is actually capable of, when supported.

Fairness in testing is fundamental, and particular care needs to be taken to ensure this in the case of young learners. The younger the learner, the less world-knowledge they have to draw on. While an adult can be expected to read about or discuss a wide range of topics, or grasp complex and abstract ideas and concepts, this is not the case for children. A child who has not personally experienced travelling, or a particular sport, may be disadvantaged in the face of a text on the subject. For the youngest children, test-makers of widely used tests, for example national tests, should carry out surveys of what has been typically covered in classrooms.

Washback is a major issue in the testing of young learners. What is tested will affect what is learnt, either by being prioritized in classroom practice, or simply by achieving more status in the minds of pupils and parents. This can be true even of a weekly class test, if it always covers the same aspect of language, and it is particularly true in the case of higher-stakes tests. Anecdotal evidence from Norway suggests that when national English writing tests were introduced in 2004, parents were conscious of an increase in the writing activity of their children in primary and secondary school, which waned from the point where these tests were dropped, and replaced by the testing of reading only, three years later. It is the responsibility of those who plan testing, to ensure that this does not adversely affect what goes on in the classroom.

The importance of good *feedback* and the sharing of *criteria* cannot be overemphasized, and as far as is appropriate in the test situation, the same principles apply to testing as to classroom/formative assessment, described in the previous section.

Some mention should be made here of how *interesting* a test should be. The short attention span of younger children, and their need for play fantasy and fun (Hasselgreen 2000: 162) puts the onus on test-makers to produce tests and tasks which engage young learners and keep their attention. Hasselgreen (2000: 264) describes a test in the skills of reading, listening, 'general language use' and writing, administered to 6th grade children (11/12 years) in Norway. The whole test set combined to make an adventure story 'The Stolen Elephant', with each skill being tested in one episode. The tests were all contained in a booklet, which was cartoon-based, and accompanied by a CD, with acting and music. The children did the test over a two-week – or four-session – period, handing the book in after each episode. Responses in the self-assessment forms (which accompanied each episode), as well as the answers pupils gave, showed the high degree of engagement and fun they had had, working through this 'story'.

The points covered above have focused to a large extent on the younger learners, children rather than teenagers. However, it would be a mistake to think that they no longer apply as children mature. Teenagers are also vulnerable and limited in what they know. They also need to know why and in what they are being tested, and how they are being judged. They need constructive feedback and support, and an interesting and engaging test is always preferable to the alternative, whatever the age. In short, what have been cited here as principles of good testing apply to both children and teenagers. Adherence to the principles, and making visible the fact that they are being adhered to, are also appreciated, and indeed expected, by that other group who are involved in the testing of young learners – their parents.

Other Assessment Issues

Computerized Testing

Language tests – particularly those conducted on a large scale – are increasingly computerized. This can be seen in the case of young learners, for example in British Council's *Aptis Teens* tests, in the Cambridge English Young Learners' tests (https://www.teachers.cambridgeesol.org/ts/exams/younglearnersandforschools) and in the Norwegian National Tests of English (http://www.udir.no/Vurdering/Nasjonale-prover/Engelsk/Engelsk/). Even at the classroom level, teachers are able to use computerized tests, for example, taken from their coursebook website, or created by themselves through their own local Internet platforms. This section will give a brief overview of some issues surrounding the use of computerized tests.

Computerized tests are probably as varied as paper tests. They can test different skills, some providing instant automatic scoring and feedback, and some adapting to the level of the learner. The European Union's DIALANG (http://dialangweb.lancaster.ac.uk) test is an early example of just how widely and flexibly the computer/Internet can be used to test languages, with all of the European Union's official languages being adaptively tested across a full range of skills and levels on the CEFR, with self-assessment and feedback built into the system.

A large-scale computerized test can be piloted widely, and the data from both piloting and test results used to ensure the quality of the tests. Where tests are scored automatically – which is quite usual for tests of receptive skills or language structures – the absence of a human rater can enhance reliability. To offset the cost of developing computerized tests, there can also be a considerable saving in paper and postage, besides using drastically fewer resources in the scoring. The formats used can have a game-like quality, with particular appeal for younger learners. Appendix C.1 shows an extract from the Norwegian National Test of English reading, 5th grade (http://www.udir.no/Vurdering/Nasjonale-prover/Engelsk/Engelsk/) where a 'click and drag' format is used. An adaptive computerized test, which directs the test-taker to a level most suited to what appears to be his/

her ability, can be used advantageously with younger learners, allowing them to use their time more effectively on tasks at a suitable level.

Concerns have been raised, however, regarding computerized tests. One such concern relates to the validity of the tests, and whether they represent a test of computer skills rather than language ability (e.g. Manger, Eikeland and Vold 2009). However, studies such as Choi, Kim and Boo (2003), have contributed to the evidence that paper-based and computerized tests of language do not measure different abilities. Another concern is whether the skill being tested, such as reading, is 'real' reading when it is done on a computer. But as an increasing amount of literacy and communicative activity takes place digitally, there seems little reason to regard computerized communication as less 'real' than 'paperized' or face-to- face communication. Jones and Brown (2011) carried out a study of the reading of e-books and paper books by 22 third grade pupils, measuring their motivation for independent reading, as well as reading comprehension. The study concluded that the format (paper or e-book) had less effect on either motivation or comprehension than the children's identification with the setting, characters and themes of the book. It is important to ensure that when designing tasks for a computerized test, real-life communication on/via computer is reflected, such as writing on a forum, as in the Aptis Teens writing test. This goes some way to combatting the concerns regarding whether the test is testing computer skills or language skills and in turn enhances the transparency of the test's purpose, as well as its validity.

Other concerns regard the limitations of computerized tests, for example, their ability to automatically assess spoken or written production in the way that a human rater would. This can be overcome by delivering the production to a rater, for example, or using such media as Skype. The format of tasks used in automatically-assessed tests, for example, of reading, may be restricted, with multiple choice answers being easier for the computer to mark than longer, more reflective answers. A word of warning should be added here concerning the creating of computerized tests by teachers or others, using an online programme, for example, with multiple-choice formats. Here the user simply has to type in the questions, with answers and distracters, and the technical side is taken care of. The pitfall is that good multiple-choice questions are notoriously difficult to make. Anyone attempting this should take precautions, such as ensuring that neither the correct answer nor any distracters 'stand out', or that the answer is obvious, or that distracters are simply not plausible. It is advisable to try these out on someone before using them; it can, in fact, be worth testing whether the right answer to a question can be chosen without reading or listening to the text it is based on!

There are also specific concerns about test security, such as the possibility of taking photos of the questions with mobile phones and distributing these widely at the click of a button, or of accessing the Internet for the answers. Measures need to be taken to prevent these breaches from occurring.

While there are many challenges remaining for the developers of computerized tests, there can be little doubt that these tests are here to stay. Meanwhile, it is up to users to understand the limitations of computerized testing, while exploiting this method's unquestionable potential.

Tasks and Young Learners

Finally, the discussion will turn to the tasks we give learners in either classroom assessment or testing. As we cannot see into the mind of learners, and are limited in how much dialogue we can have with individuals, the task is often the medium through which we see what learners know or can do. We have to put faith in tasks, to trust that they enable learners to show their language ability. Therefore, we will consider in this section the extent to which this trust may be well- or ill-founded.

Cameron (2001) gives an account of the kind of demands tasks can place on children, and correspondingly, the kind of support they may need to carry out the task. While in language assessment, we ostensibly design tasks to elicit evidence of children's linguistic ability of a particular kind, a task may fail to do this because the child lacks other abilities required to carry it out. In testing terms, this can lead to construct irrelevance variance, but it is also salient to everyday classroom assessment. Cameron identifies six types of demands placed by tasks.

1. Cognitive – for example, the child's grasp of certain concepts, which may be explicitly referred to in the task or simply taken for granted.
2. Language – in addition to the language or skill we are specifically assessing, other demands can be imposed, for example, grammatical knowledge in a task designed to test vocabulary.
3. Interactional – this can include the type of discourse, such as conversation, and the participants, such as teacher or peer.
4. Metalinguistic – this involves the language used about the task, for example, a written or spoken instruction.
5. Involvement – the degree to which the child is able to engage in the task and give it full attention.
6. Physical – this can include any actions, or extended sitting still, or motor skills needed to write or draw.

(Adapted from Cameron 2001: 25)

In designing tasks for any group of children, it is necessary to anticipate all of these demands, and as far as possible, build in support – particularly in testing. This may be brought about by using pictures to contextualize the task, for example, and by clarifying concepts which may be difficult. The language otherwise used in the task or instruction, should not be more demanding than the particular language being tested. Importantly, the kind of activity or interaction should be of the type the children are used to and able to cope with, and the tasks should as far as possible be engaging. Demonstrating an example of the task is important, or letting the children do practice tasks before a test. In classroom assessment or informal testing, it may be possible to give support to a child during the assessment, and in interpreting a poor test result, it can be useful to investigate what it was that prevented a child from performing well.

A number of developmental factors that we identified in Chapter 1 can make some tasks too demanding for young learners, even into the teenage years. The youngest children will struggle with tasks that are linked thematically and require appreciating a 'wholeness' in the set. And as they do not mentally organize concepts in the way that adults do, they may produce unexpected answers to questions that are based on this organization. For instance, if a child is given these three items: 'a toothbrush, some soap and a plate' and is asked to choose the odd one out, the answer anticipated would be the plate, as this is found in the kitchen, the other two items belonging to the bathroom. However, a child could equally choose the toothbrush based on its shape. It is long and the other two items are round.

Older children may have difficulties with tasks that require them to understand the gist of a long or complicated text. Even for young teenagers, abstract logical problems may pose difficulties; a task on grammar, requiring the rewriting of a sentence, for example, from active to passive form, can be more a test of logical reasoning than grammar. And, according to Morgan (2013), the prefrontal cortex does not fully develop until around 15 to 17 years, which has implications for the way teenagers may respond to tasks. They may struggle to understand rhetorical devices, such as irony, or make connections between complex or apparently opposing ideas.

The bottom line is, in making tasks, we need to ensure that 'irrelevant' abilities, which might be taken for granted in an adult, do not get in the way of a young learner being able to demonstrate his/her knowledge and ability in the assessment.

Conclusion

This chapter has introduced the topic of assessment. For convenience of organization, it has separately presented overviews of features of *formative assessment*, and principles of *language testing*, which may have a formative or summative purpose, and which often play a major role in classroom assessment. Some attention was also paid to the issues of computerized testing and tasks in the context of young learners.

Language testing, which will be the main subject from now on, has undergone a move from testing language points in isolation towards a task-based, communicative approach. We are less interested in simply whether a learner 'knows' a language item than whether s/he can use their language in communication. The items given in this type of test attempt, as far as possible, to simulate 'real-life' language use, in the 'skills' of reading, writing, speaking, listening, or a combination of any of these. The following four chapters will focus on these in turn. Additionally, as there can be situations where we need to know the extent to which learners' vocabulary has developed, or whether they have mastered certain grammatical forms, a further, short, chapter will follow these, on the testing of vocabulary and grammar.

In each of the chapters on specific skills, a rough pattern will be followed. After addressing some issues specific to the particular skill, or area to be tested, a model will be presented. This model will be used to describe what is involved, for example, in reading, in the context of L2 testing. The final part of each chapter will draw the threads together in a practical consideration of the actual testing of the particular skill. Here, each of our three age groups – younger and older children and teenagers – will be considered in turn, in the light of what the early chapters have revealed about the potential of each age group, and how this is related to CEFR levels.

The ordering of the chapters on skills may appear at a glance to be counter-intuitive, particularly in the case of younger learners, where there is a general perception that the oral language has primacy over the written. The ordering used here, beginning with reading and writing, was decided on for reasons of clarity of structure. Reading and writing, while not totally independent, are more easily treated as distinct activities than are speaking and listening, which most normally occur together in interaction. This being so, it was easier to apply the pattern described above for the chapters on the written skills, with those on the oral skills deviating somewhat from this pattern. A similar reasoning led to the positioning of the chapter on listening after that on speaking, while reading is treated before writing. This ordering of chapters has no intended implications for what might be considered the relative importance of skills, or the order in which they are acquired.

5   Testing Reading

This chapter on testing reading is the first of five which consider the testing of different aspects of language ability/knowledge. Chapters 5 to 8 cover 'the four skills' of reading, writing, speaking and listening, in a communicative testing context. Communicative testing involves using tasks which emulate, as far as possible, the kind of use we put our language to in 'real life', which may in fact be the classroom simulating life outside. Chapter 9 veers away from this, looking at the testing of vocabulary and grammar using minimally-communicative tasks. The word 'testing' is used consciously here, rather than 'assessment'. This does not mean that classroom assessment has been forgotten. Testing, as was pointed out in Chapter 4, constitutes an important part of informal ongoing assessment.

At this point there is a need for some clarification and tightening up of terminology. 'Task' has been used in a fairly loose, but conventional sense, involving something we ask our learners to do, in order to show their knowledge or ability. In this chapter and Chapter 8, both of which involve the receptive skills, 'task' will refer to what a learner is supposed to do in response to a text, written or spoken. The term 'item' will used to denote text-plus-task; this will be expanded upon in the course of the chapter. The word 'skill' has largely been used so far in the context of 'the four skills', as listed above. However, its normal use from now on will be reserved for a narrower concept of skills, such as cognitive skills.

The chapter will begin with a short discussion of some general issues concerning reading and its assessment, introducing a model of L2 reading. This model, together with what we have already established about young learners' L2 development, will provide the basis for a practical consideration of the testing of L2 reading, taking each age group in turn. This will take language ability and domain into account, using the CEFR levels as reference points.

Reading: Some General Issues

A number of issues tend to recur in the literature on L2 reading and its assessment. These typically include: (sub)skills, strategies and knowledge involved in reading, purposes for reading, and characteristics of a text which affect reading difficulty. Before addressing these issues, however, a much-debated topic will be taken up. As suggested in Chapter 2, L1 literacy is generally regarded as a forerunner for L2 literacy. We need to further explore whether there are grounds for claiming this, and whether good L2 reading is about being a good reader, or being good at the L2, or both.

L1 and L2 Literacy

The degree to which L1 reading skills and L2 language skills differentially contribute to L2 reading comprehension has been studied with varying results and conclusions. Alderson (2000: 23–24), acknowledges the importance of both factors, language knowledge and reading knowledge, but inclines towards the *threshold* view, which holds that below a certain linguistic (L2) threshold, L1 reading competence is unlikely to have a major effect on L2 reading. From the perspective of young learners' L2 reading, this has been researched in large-scale projects such as those reported in Van Gelderen, Schoonen, Stoel, de Glopper and Hulstijn (2007) and in Nikolov and Csapo (2010).

Van Gelderen *et al.* (2007) investigated longitudinally the L1 and L2 reading abilities of Dutch-speaking adolescents as they advanced through three years of secondary schooling, from 8th grade (aged 13–14 years), where they had had roughly 1.5 years of L2 English, through to 10th grade. They were tested on reading comprehension in both L1 and L2, as well as in a number of other areas including their knowledge of vocabulary and grammar in L1 and L2. The conclusion was that L1 reading ability was the factor which contributed most to L2 reading ability, but that, in both L1 and L2 reading, vocabulary and grammar were also contributing factors. Furthermore, it was found that the effect of the L1 reading ability gradually strengthened as the pupils matured and/or increased their L2 proficiency.

Nikolov and Csapo (2010) carried out a similar investigation on the L1 and L2 reading skills of children in Hungary, at 6th grade and 8th grade, with the level of English ranging from A1 to lower A2 on the CEFR. Among the factors that were tested, in addition to L1 and L2 reading, were L2 writing and listening as well as inductive reasoning. As opposed to Van Gelderen *et al.'s* study, L1 reading was found to be a relatively small factor in its contribution to L2 reading ability, with an effect roughly similar to that of inductive reasoning. L2 writing and listening correlated more strongly with L2 reading. By comparing the data with that of older students (10th and 12th grades), Nikolov and Csapo found that the effect of L1 reading ability decreased with age.

Thus, it seems that the evidence is not clear as to whether language ability or L1 reading ability has most effect on L2 reading. However, both these studies give support to the view that the L2 reading ability of young learners is affected to some degree by L1 literacy, even at levels as low as A1-A2 on the CEFR.

Variables Involved in Testing Reading

The (sub)skills, knowledge and strategies involved in the reading process have been identified and classified in many forms. In Alderson's (2000) presentation of various classifications of these, the quantities range from 1 to 19. These include such wide-ranging elements as decoding, automatic recognition of words, (micro)linguistic knowledge, topic familiarity, world and discourse knowledge, cognitive skills, such as inferencing, reasoning and evaluating, and metacognitive skills. While there is broad agreement that a number of skills are involved in reading, and that many of these can be trained and individually assessed (for example, as demonstrated by Grellet 1981), they are notoriously difficult to isolate and measure in the testing of reading comprehension, although it has been suggested, for example, by Alderson (2000) that this may be possible at lower proficiency levels. Van Steensel, Oostdam and van Gelderen (2013) investigated the possibility that sub-skills of reading comprehension may be separately measurable, employing specific tasks given to 200 low-achieving adolescent readers (in Dutch, mainly as L1) in the Netherlands. The tasks were intended to trigger three levels of text understanding: retrieving, interpreting and reflecting, but no evidence was found that these sub-skills were being applied separately by the test-takers. A learner can approach any test item in numerous different ways, often compensating for one less-developed skill or area of knowledge by drawing on another. What seems to be important is to ensure that our testing is so broadly based that a suitably wide range of skills and knowledge types are drawn on in the course of a test.

The characteristics of the text which affect reading difficulty, on the other hand, can be selected and controlled in testing. Alderson (2000) suggests that these include topic, content, genre, length, organization, coherence and, of course, features of the language, such as range of vocabulary and complexity of syntax. Non-verbal features of the text, such as simple illustrations or diagrams, can greatly increase the ease of the reading, and are particularly significant in the reading of children, where much of the content of a story or poem is often transmitted through illustrations. The types of reading we do, such as scanning, skimming or careful reading, are also, to some extent, distinguishable and testable in separate items.

Thus, it seems there are many variables involved in reading, and that these are classified in widely differing ways. In order to conduct any analysis of L2 reading, it is clear that having a unified way of classifying or describing each variable would be advantageous and, preferably, that these variables be put together into a single model. Khalifa and Weir's (2009: 43) model of reading exemplifies this, and will be drawn on here, in a simplified and slightly adapted form, shown in Figure 5.1. The model will be used in combination with our earlier findings, as a basis for characterizing L2 reading in the context of testing young learners at various age ranges.

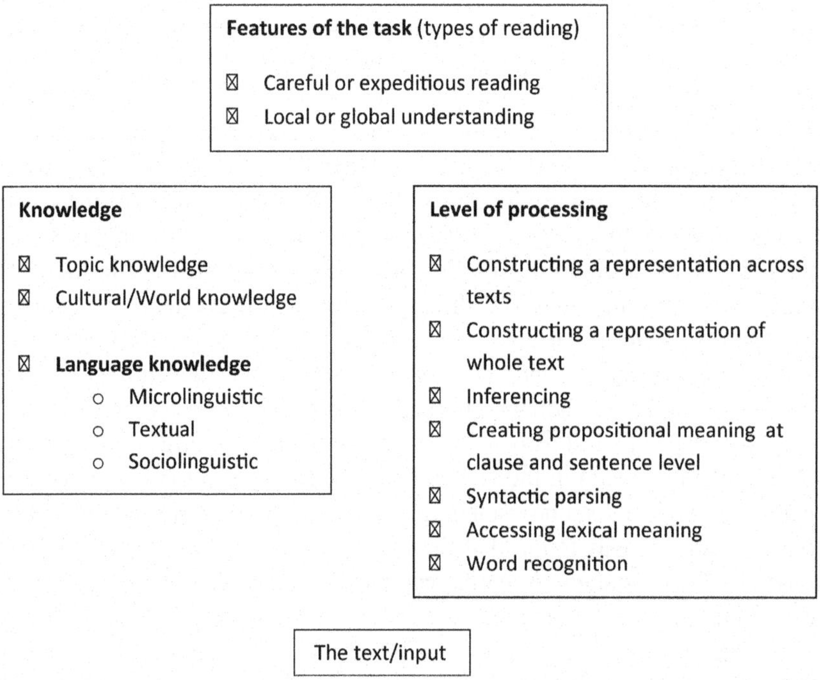

Features of the task (types of reading)

☒   Careful or expeditious reading
☒   Local or global understanding

Knowledge

☒   Topic knowledge
☒   Cultural/World knowledge

☒   **Language knowledge**
   ○   Microlinguistic
   ○   Textual
   ○   Sociolinguistic

Level of processing

☒   Constructing a representation across texts
☒   Constructing a representation of whole text
☒   Inferencing
☒   Creating propositional meaning at clause and sentence level
☒   Syntactic parsing
☒   Accessing lexical meaning
☒   Word recognition

The text/input

Figure 5.1: A model of L2 reading (adapted from Khalifa and Weir 2009: 43)

A Model of L2 Reading

The model has four basic parts, pertaining to: text/input, features of the task (type of reading), knowledge and processing. The model will be interpreted here in the context of a person doing a test item, which can be considered as a text (alongside any other visual input, such as a picture), with a task to be carried out. The task demands a certain type of reading, and requires the application of some kind of knowledge and some level of processing of what is read. Other demands of tasks salient to children, such as those cited from Cameron (2001) in the previous chapter, will not be taken up here, not being specific to the testing of reading. However, they should be taken into account when making tasks. Considerations of the format of items, and how they will be scored, will be briefly taken up later.

Texts have many features which can affect the difficulty of reading them. As mentioned in Section 5.1, these may involve aspects of the content, structure and language, as well as non-verbal features such as illustrations or diagrams. The 'readability' of texts can be gauged quite simply using specialized computer applications, and this can be used as a rough guide to difficulty, always taking into account other factors, such as topic.

The *type of reading* implied by the task can be considered in terms of two dimensions. The first concerns whether the reading required is *careful*, where the text is closely scrutinized, or *expeditious*, where the text is superficially, and ideally quickly, looked though. These can be combined with the 'location' dimension, i.e. where the information can be found: *local* or *global*. Careful reading can involve understanding particular sentences (local) or the overall text (global). Expeditious reading can involve scanning for specific information/ideas (local), and skimming to get the gist, or searching for main ideas and important detail (global).

The *knowledge* drawn on in reading consists of the topic, cultural or world knowledge we bring to the reading, as well as L2 language knowledge. The latter, following our model in Chapter 2, consists of microlinguistic knowledge (e.g. vocabulary, syntax, spelling), textual knowledge (e.g. use of connectors, genre conventions), and sociolinguistic knowledge (e.g. terms or style appropriate to the topic, addressee or genre). Strategies are not included here, as they are considered to relate to processing.

The *processing* is arranged in a hierarchy of levels, each one building on the level(s) below. The first level is *word recognition*, followed by accessing *lexical meaning*, i.e. forming some kind of understanding of the word or lexical item, which can include 'chunks', such as *football match*. This may be sufficient to carry out the task, particularly in items targeting lower proficiency levels. The next level, *syntactic parsing*, is necessary if the task involves understanding at the whole sentence or clause level; this should lead to the level of *creating a propositional meaning*, or understanding the explicit idea(s) expressed. Above this level is *inferencing*, which draws not only on knowledge from within the text itself, but also on what the reader brings to the text in the way of world or topic knowledge. This may put the reader in a position to construct a *representation of the text* as it is structured, understanding how parts may relate to each other and to the whole text, for example, cause and effects, and conclusions. The highest level of all involves relating the particular text to other texts, constructing *representation across texts.* Despite the fact the Khalifa and Weir (2009) found a degree of correspondence between the levels of proficiency in Cambridge exam tasks and the levels of processing these tasks required, there seems no reason to assume that this correspondence is absolute. The fairly simple task of comparing hotels on the Internet can involve all levels of processing. The degree of 'advancedness' involved in these levels is affected by the text(s) concerned, and the knowledge the learner brings to the text.

In the following consideration of each age group in turn, and taking into account the range of CEFR levels these groups represent, we will investigate how the parts of the model can be brought together in characterizing test items. Before embarking on this, however, there are two important aspects of a reading test item which have so far been left aside but need to be addressed, namely the format and the scoring/interpretation of scores.

Item Format

The format of an item can be described in terms of 'input' and 'expected response' (Bachmann and Palmer 1996). The input of a reading test item will typically consist of 'the text', as well as any illustrations or diagrams, instructions for the task and possibly alternative answers to choose from. In some items, the instruction itself may be the text, for example, in a lower level computerized test with pictures, the text/instruction might simply be: 'click on the apple'.

The format of the expected response, may be 'closed'. This could involve, for example, the selection of an answer, which may be verbal (e.g. multiple choice statements) or non-verbal (e.g. a picture). Closed responses may include 'actions', such as drawing lines to match objects, or dragging objects in a computerized test; they can also involve manipulating the text, such as rearranging paragraphs in a computerized test. On the other hand, the format may be 'open', normally involving a written response, ranging in length from a single word up to an essay.

Whether the test is on paper or computerized has an effect on the formats of both the input and expected response. A computerized test, as shown above, offers possibilities of dragging objects or parts of a text, and identifying text or picture by clicking, which are less easy to achieve in a paper test. On the other hand, a computerized test which is automatically scored limits the scope in eliciting open responses. Even a single-word written response can be difficult for the computer to handle, both because of potential spelling errors and because it is not always possible to predict all possible answers. This can limit the type of question that can be asked. *What, when* or *who* questions can often be answered on a computer by clicking, for example, on a name or date in the text. However, higher-order questions, such as *why* or *how,* or questions involving inferencing or evaluation, may best be served by open questions. In computer testing a solution to this can be a compromise, whereby the computer scores the closed items, while open parts are sent to 'human raters' for scoring.

Scoring/Interpreting Scores

On a test of reading, the scoring is normally done by allocating points for correct or acceptable answers, judged on set criteria in the case of open items. At its simplest, one point is allocated to each answer. Weighting may be used, allocating a higher number of points to more difficult/advanced items. The result of a test typically consists of a single score, which represents 'reading ability' however we have defined it. It may be that in a large-scale test, such as a national test, the material accompanying the test will list some sub-skills which make up this reading ability, for example, from a school curriculum. Examples of these may be *recognizing common words, understanding simple sentences* and *inferencing.* As has been pointed out here, it is notoriously difficult to test these skills in isolation. However, it is common to design a range of tasks which seem likely to target particular skills, in order to achieve a balanced test. What should be avoided is giving sub-scores based on small groups of items perceived to target sub-skills, unless this is based on careful analysis of the test data.

Care should be taken to avoid using items that depend on each other. It is always advisable to have more options than needed if matching objects or words from a set, to avoid having the 'last one left' as the obvious answer. Some computerized tests are designed to remove answer options once they have been selected, and again care must be taken to avoid the answer becoming obvious from what is left. Where written answers are required, a decision must be made regarding the 'correctness' of the language, or even whether the L1 will be permitted. In principle, to ensure a truly valid test of reading, the answer should only be judged on the extent to which it demonstrates that the test-taker had understood the content being tested.

In interpreting scores, it can be helpful to have input from the test-takers if possible, either in the form of a discussion of the answers after the test, or of self-assessment questions at the end of the test. These questions can address such issues as whether they had enough time and understood what to do, and if there were texts or tasks that they found too difficult. Young learners can also be asked whether they liked the tests and why/why not, and, importantly, what they have learned.

Testing the L2 Reading of Different Age Groups

The remainder of the chapter will be devoted to a consideration of the actual testing of L2 reading of young learners. We will look at each of our three age groups in turn. The model of reading shown in Figure 5.1 will be drawn on, in terms of the types of reading suitable for the group, the range of *knowledge* which can be expected, the levels of *processing* potentially followed and, finally, the *test items* (text + task) suitable to be given to the group. It should be pointed out that the type of reading done, the actual knowledge drawn on and the processes followed in order to carry out any task can vary from learner to learner, so that item sets should be designed to activate these widely, rather than attempting to report on them specifically. The findings on young learner development from Chapters 1 to 3 will be drawn on, particularly those concerning the CEFR levels found to be potentially reachable by the different age groups. As a prelude to this, we will examine what can be inferred for reading at the relevant CEFR levels. Levels which can be considered roughly midway between two whole CEFR levels will be referred to using the denotation *A2/B1*, etc.

CEFR Levels

Given that every age group may have learners across a range of levels of the CEFR, from A1 upwards (sometimes all in the same school class), the levels which can occur in the various age groups are defined in Table 5.1, based on what were found in Chapter 3 to be the upper levels generally attainable for the groups.

Table 5.1: The CEFR Levels Likely to Be Attainable for the Age-groups

Age groups	Range of levels likely to occur
Young children (roughly between 5/6 years and 8/9 years)	(below) A1 to A2 (Reading and writing levels dependent on the emergence of literacy)
Older children (roughly between 8/9 years and 12/13 years)	(below) A1 to B1
Teenagers (roughly between 13 and 17 years)	(below) A1 to B2 (with some exceptional older teenagers at C1).

Based mainly on the CEFR *self assessment grid for reading* (Council of Europe 2001: 26–27), the levels for reading can be characterized as:

- A1: Can read highly familiar words or phrases and very short simple sentences (pre-grammatical).
- A2: Can read very short, simple texts, including personal letters/messages; ranges of language and topics are very limited; can find specific information for example from a catalogue.
- B1: Can read straightforward texts on familiar matters, using high frequency language; can understand descriptions of events, wishes and feelings in personal letters.
- B2: Can read texts of varied genres; can understand the writer's viewpoints and attitudes.
- C1: Can understand long and complex texts, appreciating differences in style.

It should be noted that these levels are defined in the CEFR descriptors largely in terms of the text that can be 'read'. There is little mention of what learners *do* with texts, and particularly those that may be beyond the level they are 'at'. While someone's French may not be much higher than A1, they can probably, if the need arises, make some attempt at getting the gist of a shorter French text, using whatever language/topic knowledge and skills they possess.

A study on what readers can 'do' with texts at different CEFR levels was carried out by Hasselgreen and Helness (2014) and formed a presentation at the 2014 European Association for Language Testing and Assessment's (EALTA) Conference The study was based on item data gathered from the testing of over 50,000 pupils on the Norwegian National Tests of English (NNTE) (http://www.udir.no/Vurdering/Nasjonale-prover/Engelsk/Engelsk/), 5th grade (approximately 10 years). A standard-setting procedure involving 15 raters was carried out, to find cut-off scores on the whole test for key CEFR levels and half levels. The items were qualitatively analysed by the researchers to find characteristics of items ' doable', defined as having p values >0.66, i.e. answered correctly by two out of three children in the 'populations' assigned to the different CEFR levels/half levels. Table 5.2 shows the results of the study, indicating a relationship between CEFR level, text, task and process.

Younger Children: Aged 5/6 to 8/9 Years (A1 to A2)

There will be children in this group who are approaching A1, or on 'level A0', and it is important that they are given a chance to manage some simple tasks, for example by recognizing cognates of familiar L1 words, or well-known international words, like *hamburger*. This is also the age at which

Table 5.2: Characteristics of Items 'doable' at a Range of CEFR Levels, by 10 Year-olds

CEFR level	Reading tasks doable
A1	Can identify very familiar words /fixed phrases with support of picture/physical context, even in longer texts.
A1/A2	Can identify familiar words/very simple clauses with support of picture/physical context, even in longer texts.
A2	Can create meaning from individual clauses/sentences, including in longer texts, not simply dependent on word/phrase recognition.
A2/B1	Can make connections between individual clauses/sentences. Can create meaning from series of sentences.
Lower B1	Can create meaning and make inferences from whole texts, beyond the level of a series of adjacent sentences.

Adapted from Hasselgreen and Helness, EALTA Conference presentation, 2014

children's L1 reading skills are just emerging, and this has to be taken into account when giving tests or interpreting scores.

Type of Reading
Texts for this age group tend to be short, and the distinctions between careful and expeditious and between local and global reading are generally trivial. However, even a reader around A1 may find the correct answer to a question on a longer text, ostensibly requiring careful reading, by simply skimming for words they know.

Knowledge
The lexical knowledge at level A1 is limited to a range of very immediate words and learned 'chunks' (e.g. *my name is…*) and phrases, while at A2 it has expanded to cover a limited core of everyday topics of interest to the child. Syntactic knowledge is starting to emerge around A2. The world knowledge of children at any level is usually very limited, and topic knowledge cannot be taken for granted, so they should be given support from pictures. Text genre knowledge is limited to a basic, linear structure in short texts, or predictable structures associated with familiar text types, such as described below.

Levels of Processing
While a child around level A1 may not be able to process at a higher level than lexical access, from around A2 children should be able to establish the propositional meaning of sentences. This is, of course, dependent on the text, and how familiar and predictable it is. On reading the birthday party

invitation shown in Figure 5.2, most children in cultures where such invitations are common will be able to manage to answer specific questions such as *What day is the party?*, by skimming the text to locate the relevant information. It is reasonable to suppose that they will also manage to process this simple text as a whole, making a mental representation, and clearly understanding how the parts fit into the whole, even carrying out some very simple inferencing, for example, *Who has their birthday this week?*

Test Items

The texts that younger children can be given are related to their age and interests, their language ability and the domain of reading they are used to. The texts described as 'readable' at the lowest CEFR levels consist of well-known words and phrases in isolation, or in the context of simple sentences (around level A1), gradually bringing in short simple texts on familiar matters (around level A2). Pictures feature highly, as they do in many texts read by this age group, and texts normally range in length from a word or phrase to two or three sentences. The vocabulary is generally concrete, and syntax and morphology, including links within and between sentences, are simple. Themes typically covered are those that children tend to know well, such as colours, pets, weather, school, or family. Although the structure is normally straightforward, the text 'genre' can vary a lot, including simple stories, descriptions, postcards, mobile phone text messages (SMS), party invitations, calendars, notes and clocks. The functions of the texts used at this stage are mainly to give information and/or instructions, and as far as possible, to entertain. Although it would be possible for children around A2 to do some simple tasks on texts longer than those which the CEFR suggests for this level, it is probably inadvisable to give long, difficult-looking texts to younger children, since they may find them demotivating and demanding of more attention than they are prepared to give.

To ensure that all children in this age range can experience success, some items need to be targeted at the lowest level of all, where identifying a word is all that is expected. Tasks that involve matching pictures with words or short sentences, where the clues are in the vocabulary, are suitable for A1 pupils, who can scan a sentence to find a word they know. Simple instructions, especially on computer, such as *Put the cat on the tractor*, can be fun and are manageable for children whose L1 words for *cat* and *tractor* are similar to the L2 (which is also a consideration in making the items). As they increase their vocabulary they can manage tasks of the kind shown in Figure 5.2, which involves finding the label *chicken* and dragging it to the picture (see Norwegian Diagnostic Test of English, 3rd grade/Utdannings-direktoratet, http://www.udir.no/Vurdering/Kartlegging-gs/).

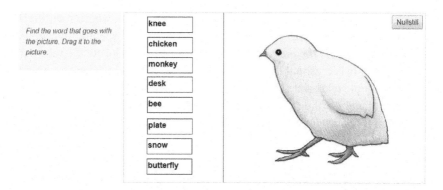

Figure 5.2: Example item from the Norwegian diagnostic test of reading, 8/9 years, 2015 (© Norwegian Directorate for Education and Training [Utdanningsdirektoratet])

Children approaching A2 can gradually manage tasks which require using the syntax/morphology of a sentence to work out the meaning, and therefore tasks should be given in which the vocabulary alone cannot yield the answer. The children may also use semantic connections (e.g. hungry – eat) to give a correct response, drawing on a widening vocabulary rather than syntax.

A text such as the party invitation, shown in Figure 5.3, can be used with simple questions such as *who, what, where and* and *when,* in the range A1 to A2.

Tasks such as choosing the correct sentence half to complete a sentence or the correct phrase to place within a sentence are also suitable around A2, where the correct answer is determined by understanding the whole sentence, and not individual words. This is exemplified in Figure 5.4 below. The first is an upper A1 task, as it can be answered by understanding some common lexical items alone. This is in contrast to the second example, at level A2, where an understanding of the sentence as a whole is required to answer correctly.

The items shown here illustrate the progression of reading as the CEFR levels advance and the fact that it is possible to test reading without the need for lengthy texts, at lower levels in particular.

It should be mentioned here that many of the texts suggested are rather culture-specific (pets, parties, farms, even weather). This is something that has to be taken into account with young learners, in the interest of fairness, and emphasizes the importance of illustrations, to help provide a context, and to compensate for a lack of personal or cultural knowledge of the topic.

Figure 5.3: Party invitation text – for items at A1 to A2

(strong A1 task)   Rubric:
Read the sentence and choose the correct missing word.

Every year we go on holiday in a quiet place. This year we stayed _____ for a week.

---

a) in the country   b) at a party   c) in a mall   d) in a city

---

(A2 task)   Rubric:
Read the sentences and choose the correct missing phrase.

After school, all of Tom's friends went to his house. They played _____ as the weather was too nice to stay inside.

---

a)   computer games b) football c) cards d) board games

Figure 5.4: Gap-filling items at levels upper A1 and A2

Older Children: Aged 8/9 to 12/13 years (A1 to B1)

The test items described here assume that the children being tested span the whole range from around A1 to B1. This may not always be the appropriate range, and those making tests/items will have to consider the range likely to be represented by the test-takers.

Type of Reading
Items for this age group can be given requiring all types of reading: careful/expeditious and local/global.

Knowledge
The knowledge brought to the tasks will be greater for older children than for younger, in terms of world knowledge and the range of topics assumed to be familiar. Older children can also be expected to have some grasp of abstract ideas, as well as a degree of logical reasoning skills and the ability to see a 'wholeness' created by texts or parts of a text. They are also better able to get the overall gist of a straightforward text. Language knowledge will depend on the CEFR level of the child, with those at the B1 end of the continuum having a sufficient grasp of basic grammar and vocabulary to 'get by' in most texts made up of everyday, neutral, unspecialized language.

Levels of Processing
As in the case of the younger children, all processes can potentially be triggered in these children from A2 upwards, depending on the task and the complexity and length of the text. In a long and fairly complex text, children from about A2 may be able to build propositional meaning at the sentence or paragraph level, while those bordering on B1 may build a representation of a whole, longer text.

Test Items
The texts used with older children normally include some short simple ones, as described for younger children, but tend to have fewer single-word texts, which can appear 'babyish', rather employing simple sentences containing a 'clue' word. Longer 'B1-type' texts (e.g. up to two or three paragraphs) can also be used, where the language is not restricted to simple forms, having more complex sentences, and using a range of common connectors and verb tenses. The vocabulary is more abstract than for younger children. Texts, as well as being informative, instructive, and entertaining, can also be expressive of feelings and wishes, for example, in messages such as emails. Themes for this age group go beyond what is 'everyday', but the use of pictures is still beneficial, providing some contextual support where

topic knowledge cannot be assumed. Text types, as for younger children, can vary widely, although the structure of the texts remains straightforward. A test given to Norwegian 11/12 year-olds consisted of an adventure story, *The Stolen Elephant* (cited in Hasselgreen 2000), in four episodes, with the reading test as Episode 1. This test used a variety of text genres, such as an entry from a child's diary and a newspaper report giving an account of the disappearance of the elephant with a description of three suspects.

Items can be designed to challenge all relevant levels, and, as a whole, need to be captivating. In *The Stolen Elephant* reading test (Hasselgreen 2000), the tasks on the newspaper report about the theft included a set of true false statements, ranging from those requiring skimming for gist *(An elephant has been stolen)*, or understanding a sentence *(The elephant was stolen from a zoo)*, to those requiring inferencing from the whole text *(The elephant's life is in danger)*. Another task in this test was to identify the suspects from a series of pictures, involving very careful reading of descriptions.

An A1-level item involving sentence/picture matching, with the clue in a single word, *yellow*, is shown in Figure 5.5, an item taken from the Norwegian National Tests of English (NNTE) reading for 10 year-olds. As the original colour is not visible in the figure here, letters are used to help the reader identify the correct picture, which in this case is d.

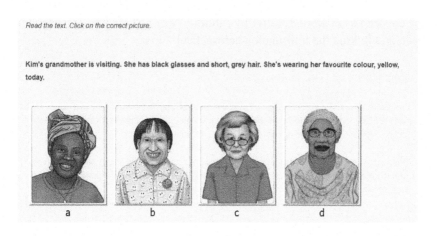

Read the text. Click on the correct picture.

Kim's grandmother is visiting. She has black glasses and short, grey hair. She's wearing her favourite colour, yellow, today.

a   b   c   d

Figure 5.5: A1 Item from the NNTE reading test for 10 years olds (© Norwegian Directorate for Education and Training, https://pgsc.udir.no/kursweb/content?contentItemId=40429207&marketplaceId=624075&selectedLanguageId=1)

Items targeting level A2 demand basic syntactic/morphological knowledge as well as a widened vocabulary base. They can exploit the children's increased reasoning ability, for example, by requiring them to compare a number of possible interpretations of a text, which vary only in some detail.

This is exemplified in the click picture item shown in Figure 5.6 in which a three-sentence text is to be matched with one of four pictures; much of the vocabulary in the text could apply to several of the pictures, and the sequence of sentences has to be read carefully to solve the problem.

Read the text. Click on the correct picture.

An English map maker is believed to have been the first to start selling this item, in the mid-1700s. Generally the pieces are made of cardboard now, but at first they were made of wood. It contains many small pieces that must be put together to make a complete picture.

Figure 5.6: A2-level item from the NNTE reading test for 10 year-olds (© Norwegian Directorate for Education and Training [Utdanningsdirektoratet])

In the *multiple choice* task shown in Figure 5.7, the answer can be found by children from around A2/B1 by carefully reading both paragraphs in this text, and linking the information across them.

Read the text. Click on the correct answer.

Thousands of years ago, there were no towns and villages, and no farms. People just moved from place to place, looking for food. They killed wild animals and collected plants for food. Meat was cooked over fires, which kept everybody safe and warm at the same time.

When people discovered that they could tame some animals, they could stay in one place and didn't have to move around any more. So they built real houses and set up fences around the farms to keep the animals there. They had food right where they lived.

How did they find food thousands of years ago?

- ⊙ They hunted animals.
- ⊙ They grew the plants.
- ⊙ They sold the animals.
- ⊙ They bought the food.

Figure 5.7: A2/B1-level item from the NNTE reading test for 10 year-olds (© Norwegian Directorate for Education and Training [Utdanningsdirektoratet])

A more difficult task, managed mainly by children around lower B1, required creating meaning from a whole text, consisting of a series of paragraphs, such as that shown in Figure 5.8.

Read the text. Click on the correct answer.

Alice loves to bake cakes. Alice's brothers, Sam and Oliver, have hobbies that are very different from hers. They love to play video games and watch movies. But their favourite hobby is playing pranks on their sister. This drives her crazy!

One day Alice was baking a birthday cake for their father. After tasting the batter, she realized that her brothers had switched the salt and the sugar! Alice decided that she would find a great way to pay them back.

Later that evening, when the boys were busy playing video games in the basement, she went into their bedroom. She set the alarm clock to go off at 5 am. But Alice decided this was not enough. Next she snuck into their bathroom and poured blue food colouring into their shampoo. She knew that, having woken up so early, they wouldn't notice that the shampoo was blue.

Quite a sight met Alice in the kitchen the next morning. Two tired boys with blue hair sat at the table having their breakfast. Alice and her parents couldn't stop laughing.

Why are Sam and Oliver tired?

- They had played too many video games.
- They had stayed up late watching movies.
- They had been woken up very early.
- They had washed their hair to many times.

Figure 5.8: Lower B1-level item from the NNTE reading for 10 year-olds (© Norwegian Directorate for Education and Training [Utdanningsdirektoratet])

It must be emphasized that even with fairly long, complex texts, a task can be given which is 'doable' at around level A1. This is illustrated in Appendix C.2, where the task can be done by skimming the text and accessing the lexical item 'chocolate cake' (which is almost identical to the Norwegian 'sjokolade kake').

Teenagers: Aged 12/13 to 17 Years (A1 to B2) (Potentially C1)

This section will focus on testing students at CEFR levels of B1 and above, as the lower levels have been covered by what has already been presented for the younger age groups, with the reminder that 'babyish' items should be avoided. It should be noted that this does not mean that it is assumed that teenagers are at B1+ levels only. Their levels are dependent upon their exposure to English prior to secondary school; in many countries teenagers are commonly below B1.

Type of Reading
Items requiring all types of reading: careful/expeditious and local/global can be used with this age group.

Knowledge
The knowledge brought to their reading will grow as teenagers progress towards the adult world. They can deal with increasingly abstract subjects and a wider range of topics. From around B1 they will have a sufficiently large vocabulary to deal with a wide range of longer texts, and will be able to cope with gradually more advanced syntax and morphology, recognizing main ideas within and across paragraphs.

Levels of Processing
Most levels of processing can be triggered at this age. Those students who are below B1, when confronted with longer texts, may struggle to construct a representation at the level of the whole text, while those at B2/C1 level, should be able to construct intertextual level representations even in longer texts.

Test Items
The texts which can be used with teenagers cover a wider variety of topics and genres than those used for younger children and the cognitive demand can be greater, especially when dealing with higher levels, such as B2/C1. Around B1, topics should be kept to what can be expected to be familiar. But even around C1, test-takers of this age cannot be expected to cope with an unlimited variety of texts or topics. Difficulty can be built into the task, rather than the text, which ideally will be of the kind that teenagers are normally exposed to. A report on the performance and testing of a new game or piece of technology could be within the realm of a teenager around B2 to C1. Other examples include school magazine articles, Internet blogs, high school textbook entries, diary entries, instructional materials and newspaper articles.

As in the case of younger children, teenagers respond well to engaging or entertaining texts and tasks. The item shown in Appendix C.3, from *Aptis for Teens*, which is aimed at careful global reading around level B1, exemplifies this. Here four short excerpts from interviews with teenagers are presented, in the style of a school magazine. The fact that the speakers in the texts are from the same age group as the test-takers should have appeal, as learners in this age group are typically interested in the experiences and views of their peers. The task is to decide which speaker had which opinion. There are more questions than there are speakers, so that some of the speakers will be associated with more than one answer. The interview texts are quite short but the texts must all be read to ascertain who said what, requiring careful reading across sentences and inferencing.

A more difficult *Aptis for Teens* item, aimed around B2, is shown in Appendix C.4. This item is based on a longer text of about 700 words, as opposed to the shorter, B1 interview excerpts described above. Both expeditious reading and careful global reading are required here to match topic headings to paragraphs. This is not a simple word-matching task, as might be required at lower levels, where the words in the heading would be represented almost verbatim in the paragraph. Here, the headings refer to the overall content of the paragraph, and as some topics transcend paragraph boundaries, careful reading is necessary to make the right choices.

Conclusion

This chapter began with an introduction to general issues related to the testing of reading, such as the role of L1 literacy and the testability of (sub) skills, as well as a consideration of item formats and scoring. A model of reading was presented, based on that proposed by Khalifa and Weir (2009: 43). This model was then drawn on as the basis for addressing the testing of L2 reading at different stages. Taking each age group in turn, and using the conclusions from Chapter 3 which relate age groups to CEFR levels, an analysis was presented of the kind and degree of knowledge we could assume the test-takers to have, the levels of processing we could expect the readers to go through and the types of test item (text + task) which would be suitable to use.

Certain issues were highlighted concerning the testing of reading in young learners. These included the extent to which those being tested are literate in their L1, which has shown to affect L2 reading comprehension. This is a developmental issue, as well as one of educational/social context. Reading tests for the younger learners must take into account their limited type and range of vocabulary and their syntactic and morphological knowledge, as well as the fact that their world/topic knowledge is generally limited to their personal experience of/interest. They are also less able to stay focused on a task for long or to see the wholeness in a task with several parts.

As the children mature, all these areas of knowledge expand. However, even as teenagers they are limited in their understanding of the most complex connectors, as well as such devices as irony. Teenagers can cope with longer texts, but still respond best to those relating to their own peer groups and the kind of topics and genres they are most familiar with and captivated by.

An issue which is critical in testing younger and older learners is pitching the level of a test so that it reflects the range of ability/knowledge of the test-takers. While adults often learn languages in groups of a similar proficiency, and will go in for tests geared to this level, children will typically be learning and tested in year groups, and may span a huge range of ability/knowledge. This puts the onus on test-makers to cater for whatever range is intended to be represented by the test, however wide this may be. Reading-test items should reflect this. This can be done to some extent by using a range of texts of different difficulty. However, a lot can be done to ensure a range of item difficulty by presenting tasks on one and the same text, which demand differing levels of knowledge and processing.

Many of the issues relating to testing reading also relate to the subject of the next chapter: testing writing.

6   Testing Writing

Writing is very different from reading, not least where testing is concerned. In testing reading, a receptive skill, we can present a text and a task, and hope that readers will use what knowledge and ability they possess to go through certain processes to reach the right answer. Unless we investigate further, for example, in following up the test results with the learner, we have only the answer to judge by. On the basis of a single answer, we cannot draw any definite conclusions about the knowledge and ability of a test-taker, or the processes gone through to reach the answer. We normally base the test result on the number of items answered correctly, and in a reliable and valid test, this generally seems to work.

In testing writing, a productive skill, this situation is turned on its head. Provided we have tasks which give test-takers the optimal chance to show what they can do, and good criteria to judge what is written, a test response can tell us a great deal about a person's ability and knowledge. In this chapter, we will start by presenting a model of L2 writing, discussing the processes and the knowledge involved in writing. This will lead us into a discussion on the criteria for judging writing, including a summary of the way the CEFR describes writing development across levels. This will be followed by a practical consideration of tasks, which will be the main focus in the section on the testing of L2 writing at different ages. Criteria are discussed before tasks here, as it is only by knowing what we are looking for in the writing that we can create tasks that give us evidence of this. In reality, tasks and criteria tend often to be developed hand in hand, each influencing the other.

A Model of L2 Writing

Weigle (2002) presents and discusses a number of models that attempt to describe writing in the first language. These include Bereiter and Scardamalia's (1987) two-part model of *knowledge telling* and *knowledge transformation* (Weigle 2002: 33–34). Knowledge telling refers to the kind of writing which simply involves relating what we know or think in writing, rather than to a partner in conversation. Weigle (2002: 31) maintains that most writing done by children and adolescents is of this type. Knowledge transformation is more complex, since the writer changes or develops his/her own knowledge as the writing proceeds, solving problems relating to both the content and the discourse. This may occur in the writing of teenagers, for example, in persuasive or argumentative texts. Thus, both types of writing may be carried out by young learners, and a model of young learner writing should accommodate both. What is common to the two parts of Bereiter and Scardamalia's model is the fact that they contain the basic components of *task* (assignment), *content knowledge, discourse knowledge* and *processes* gone through in carrying out the task. This will be the basis for the model of L2 writing used here, with the knowledge component extended to cover L2 language knowledge. The model is presented in Figure 6.1.

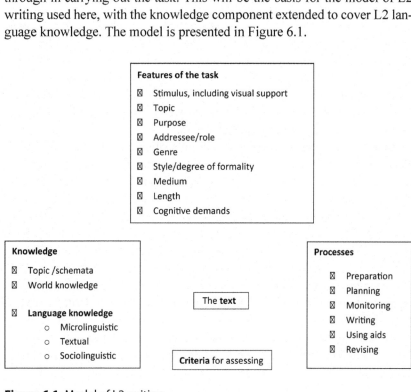

Figure 6.1: Model of L2 writing

The *features of the task* shown in our model are largely based on those presented by Weigle (2002: 63), although the *criteria* dimension has been placed separately in our model. In addition, *the text* has been included in our model, as it is the text itself, the product, which will be the outcome of the processes, and is the object to be assessed.

This model will be used in our discussion of L2 writing in the testing context. The task is designed to give the test-taker the opportunity to go through the relevant processes to create a text which demonstrates that s/he has the knowledge/abilities being assessed. The features shown here represent the demands made of the writer. These may be explicitly stated, such as the purpose and addressee, or implicitly suggested, such as the degree of formality. They also include the cognitive demands, which are unstated. The criteria for assessment will largely reflect the knowledge component of the model, but may also refer to the extent to which the task is carried out, and in some cases may refer to the processes gone through. Processes and knowledge will be examined first followed by some discussion of criteria and an age-related characterization of tasks.

Processes

The processes are expressed in a simplified way in our model, focusing on those which are considered most relevant to a discussion on testing, particularly the variables that can be controlled to some extent in the testing situation. Preparation for a writing test can come in many forms. It is well documented (e.g. Drew and Sørheim 2009) that children benefit from discussing a theme or brainstorming for ideas in advance of writing. In tests for older children and teenagers, preparation may occur through reading prior to the test or through information gathering, for example, using the Internet.

A writing test may occur as a follow-up to a series of activities, as in the case of *The Stolen Elephant* (Hasselgreen 2000), where it was possible to refer back to material during the writing. Processes such as planning, monitoring, and revising may depend on the time allowed for the test, and whether the writing is to be done in stages, with drafts being reworked before the final product is delivered. There is also a great difference between writing on paper and on computer, where revising may go on all the time. It can be eye-opening to watch children writing on computers, seeing them dive into a task, often with little planning, then suddenly erase everything and start again.

In general, whatever the medium of writing, the more formal or 'external' a test is, the more the writing processes are likely to be carried out unassisted, drawing exclusively on the competence of the writer. On the other hand, in classroom testing, and particularly in the case of younger learners, the prime interest may be in what the child has the potential to do in interaction with an adult, following Vygotskyan principles. The use of dictionaries in tests, or other aids, such as asking the teacher for spellings or words, also differs widely across situations and cultures. Younger children may come to a halt if they do not know a word, so it can be helpful for the teacher to write the word at the bottom of the page for the child to copy. This way the teacher has a record of what was the child's own work, and where s/he had help. Here again, however, writing on computer will affect the situation, with spell checks and grammar checks available, and this needs to be taken into account in a specific test.

The decisions regarding the amount of help given can also hinge on the purpose of the test. If the teacher/tester needs to know exactly what the learners know unassisted, for example, for diagnostic or placement purposes, it may be best to let the child proceed unaided, and rather use a follow-up session to give whatever help is considered useful.

Knowledge

Knowledge here, in addition to language knowledge, includes world knowledge as well as knowledge of the topic and any schemata associated with the topic, i.e. a mental representation of the situation. It also includes knowledge of the kind of discourse typically related to the topic. In the case of writing, communicative language knowledge, defined in Chapter 2, includes: *microlinguistic knowledge,* for example of vocabulary, morphology, syntax, spelling and punctuation; *textual knowledge*, for example of the use of connectors, or structures belonging to different genres; and *sociolinguistic knowledge*, for example of the way the language is typically or appropriately used in the particular situation/genre. All of these types of knowledge increase in breadth and depth as children and teenagers mature.

The knowledge we are testing in any writing test is fundamental to the criteria for assessment, which will be discussed in some detail next.

Criteria for Judging Writing

The criteria for assessing writing may involve knowledge other than linguistic, such as topic knowledge. Aspects of the presentation, such as layout on a computer screen or handwriting, may also be judged, as may be the degree of fulfilment of the actual tasks given. The extent to which aspects such as these are included in the criteria for assessment depends on the individual testing situation and how the construct of what is being tested is defined. If the process of writing is of primary interest, aspects of the process may also be reflected in the criteria. What is most central to the criteria for testing of L2 writing, however, is the knowledge of the language, as described above, and the ability to use it in writing, as evidenced in the text produced.

The extent to which young learners can be expected to possess and use this language knowledge in their writing is dependent on not only their level of proficiency in the L2, but also on their age. Younger learners are limited with respect to the type of vocabulary they can use, as well as the complexity of syntax and morphology. They are familiar with only a limited range of genres, and are generally not able to adapt their language to a wide range of situations. However, since young people are increasingly using a range of media to 'chat' to each other, they should show awareness, even in the upper primary school, that the way they 'text' their friends, for example, is different from the way they normally write an assignment at school.

The criteria for assessing writing are normally arranged in scales showing a range of levels. The aspects of language knowledge/ability discussed above are commonly reflected in scales for assessing L2 writing, as exemplified in Weigle (2002), and may be holistic, with a single scale, or analytic, with a number of separate scales, such as that exemplified in Table 6.1, which shows a scale which might be used in the classroom assessment/testing of older children.

The levels in this scale are not given any absolute value or linked to any external scale; the terms *upper, middle* and *lower level* are included for clarity, and not intended to 'label' the piece of writing. The descriptors are positive even at the lowest level, based on whatever knowledge or ability has been demonstrated in the text. The teacher can create a profile of the child's writing using this form, highlighting appropriate descriptors, which can be taken from a variety of levels. This can be used as the basis for feedback to the pupil, and as a record, to show progress. As in the case of any scale used for assessment, efforts should be made to ensure consistent use of the scale.

The Aptis Teens' scales for assessing the writing of teenagers are presented in Appendix B.2. These scales are aligned to the CEFR, and thus have 'absolute values' for the levels. Moreover, the scales divide each CEFR level into two sub-levels, for example A1.1 and A1.2. There is also a level termed A0.

What the Aptis Teens' scales and the scale in Table 6.1 have in common are the elements focused on: *vocabulary, grammar, spelling, punctuation, structure, organization* and *cohesion. Complexity, accuracy* and *appropriacy* are referred to in both. The Aptis scale includes the degree of relevance of the text to the task/topic, while the scale shown in Table 6.1 awards a 'bonus' for willingness to communicate.

The focus in this section will be on general criteria for what constitutes good L2 writing, at a range of proficiency levels and adapted for age. As we have already established a link between age groups and CEFR levels, we will begin by examining how CEFR descriptors may provide a starting point for defining criteria for writing ability at a range of levels and ages.

Table 6.1: Criteria for Assessing the Writing of Older Children (8/9 to 12/13 years) (Adapted from Hasselgreen and Drew 1999)

Communication BONUS	The pupil has really tried to communicate a message, using whatever language s/he possesses.
UPPER LEVEL	
Organization	The writing is ordered in a structured logical way, appropriate for the kind of text. There is a 'thread' running through the text, with connectors such as *after, later*. Some paragraphing may support this.
Sentencing	Some complex sentences are used, with a range of conjunctions such as *who, if, when*.
Grammar	Most basic grammar structures are used fairly correctly. It is always clear what is 'meant' in the sentence.
Words and phrases	The vocabulary is varied and at times idiomatic and appropriate to the topic of genre. Adjectives and adverbs add some 'colour' to the text.
Spelling and punctuation	Most common words are spelt correctly, and basic punctuation is used appropriately.
MIDDLE LEVEL	
Organization	There is an attempt to structure the text, and the reader is able to see some logic in the sequence of the writing.
Sentencing	Sentences are generally simple, or with clauses linked by connectors such as *and, or* and *then*. Occasional complex sentences may be used, for example, linked with *because*.
Grammar	There are signs that the pupil is aware of the most basic structures, even though there is not complete control of these.
Words and phrases	The vocabulary is sufficient to get the message across in a simple way.
Spelling and punctuation	The spelling is good enough for the text to be read and understood without much difficulty. Capital letters and full stops are usually used to indicate the boundaries of sentences.
LOWER LEVEL	
Organization	Some ideas are presented, even though these are not organized in a structured way.
Sentencing	Words and phrases are sometimes linked, for example, by *and*. Some simple sentences may be used, usually with learnt patterns.
Grammar	Some grammatical structures are used, even though these are mainly in learnt phrases.
Words and phrases	Some common words and phrases are used, to convey some simple ideas.
Spelling and punctuation	The spelling can be understood with effort, by someone who knows the pupil's L1. Capital letters and full stops may sometimes be used in the right places.

The CEFR (Council of Europe 2001) has several scales which, in combination, shed light on what may be criteria for good writing at the various levels. These include the *self-assessment grid* (2001: 26–27), *linguistic ability* (2001: 110–18), and scales specific to writing, e.g. the scales for *overall written production* (2001: 61), *creative writing* (2001: 62), *written interaction* and *correspondence* (2001: 83) and *reports and essays* (2001: 62). Between them, these scales not only provide descriptions of the elements presented above, but also present a progression in the genres and types of texts produced. A summary of what emerges from these CEFR scales for writing is provided in Table 6.2, which presents an overview of key features across the levels A1 to C1.

While the top row in Table 6.2 is mainly of relevance to specific tasks, which will be discussed further, the remaining rows demonstrate a progression of features which could be incorporated in criteria for assessing writing in general, regardless of task, and indeed which can be seen to share many elements of the scales discussed above (Aptis Teens; and Hasselgreen and Drew 1999). It has been established in Chapter 3 that approximate 'ceilings' on the CEFR levels seem to exist for each age group: younger children: A2, older children: B1, teenagers: B2 or possibly C1. Therefore, scales specifically intended to be used with these age groups would not normally contain descriptors for levels much above these, although some provision might be made for children who appear to be beyond the highest level expected, and at the same time not able to fulfil the requirements for the subsequent levels, for reasons of cognitive maturity, for example by approximating an A2+ level for younger children.

This restricted range of levels for younger learners is illustrated by the Assessment of Young Learner Literacy (AYLLIT) scale of descriptors, shown in Appendix B.1, for use with older children, whose natural CEFR ceiling can be considered around B1. The AYLLIT project (Hasselgreen, Kaledaite, Maldonado Martin and Pizorn 2011) was a European Centre for Modern Languages (ECML) project conducted in upper primary school classes in Lithuania, Spain, Slovenia and Norway. The writing part of this longitudinal study was conducted over two years, with the aim of providing teachers with tools for assessing the L2 writing of primary school children. The children in the project wrote to each other, beginning with simple descriptions of themselves and their towns, and culminating with accounts of events such as Christmas and summer holidays. The writing (first draft) was closely studied for features which emerged as the children progressed through whole and half levels of the CEFR, and this formed the basis of descriptors at seven levels, from 'approaching A1' to 'above B1'. The categories used in the scale are: *Overall structure and range of information,*

Table 6.2: Overview of Features of L2 Writing Across the Levels A1 to C1 in the CEFR

	A1	A2	B1	B2	C1
Genre/Rhetorical function	Very basic information, e.g. in forms.	Simple notes and personal letters, and very simple poems. Simple short description, including events.	Letters, stories. Description of events and feelings in some detail.	Essays, reports Evaluating, arguing. Relating to other's views.	Widely varied. Expanding and supporting viewpoints at some length.
Sentencing/structure	Isolated words and phrases.	Series of short simple phrases, sentences. Simple connectors.	Straightforward connected texts Linear sequence.	Clear detailed texts, highlighting points and relating parts.	Clearly structured complex texts.
Appropriacy/Adapting style	-	-	Expression in 'natural' register.	Formal and informal.	Style appropriate to reader.
Vocabulary	ID details. Basic repertoire.	Elementary vocabulary for everyday needs.	Sufficient to express self on most relevant or familiar matters.	Good range, although some errors and gaps.	Broad range, good command. Occasional slips.
Grammar	Limited learnt structures.	Some simple structures correct but basic errors occur.	Reasonably accurate common structures. Errors do not normally obscure message.	Relatively high degree control.	Consistent high degree of accuracy.
Spelling/punctuation	Can copy familiar words.	Reasonable phonetic accuracy in known words.	Accurate enough to be followed on the whole.	Mainly accurate, some L1 influence.	Accurate apart from occasional slip.

Sentence structure and grammatical accuracy, Vocabulary and choice of phrase, and *Misformed words and punctuation.* At the lowest end of the scale, these categories are conflated.

A scale such as the AYLLIT scale can also be used with the youngest children, omitting the highest bands. Teachers using the scale for feedback and record-keeping can remove bands that are too high or low to be relevant or useful, and add a comment based on the profile emerging from the scale, with specific reference to the child's strengths or weaknesses. In classroom assessment (for which it was primarily intended) the resulting profile will be regarded as just that, showing strengths and weaknesses in the writing. As a rule of thumb, if a level has to be decided on, it should take into account the 'average' rough levels shown in the profile, using 'pluses' and 'minuses' if helpful.

Testing the L2 Writing of Different Age Groups

In this section, the main focus will be on features of tasks appropriate for young learners in different age groups. The tasks given in a test of writing should, in combination, allow the writers to show that they have the knowledge or abilities referred to in the criteria. When the learners being tested represent a range of levels, which is often the case, it is worth giving a selection of tasks 'targeting' the full range of relevant levels. A postcard may only provide evidence that a child has reached A2, while the same child may show, through a story, that s/he is in fact at B1. On the other hand, a teenager at a level below B1 would struggle to write a letter to a newspaper, and may possibly give up, making a better shot of an email describing his/her school. When judging an individual's responses to tasks, it is advisable to look for any evidence in the set of responses that the criteria for a certain level have been met. It may be that only one of the tasks allows the writer to show his/her full potential.

The model of writing in Figure 10 lists several features of tasks: *stimulus/visual support, topic, purpose, addressee, genre, style/degree of formality, medium, length* and *cognitive demands.* These will be referred to when relevant in the age-related discussion below. As a rule, while the importance of visual support generally decreases with age/level, there is an increase in what is demanded of length, stylistic variation and degree of formality, as well as the range of topics, purposes and addressees. A set of task should vary these features sufficiently to show whether the test-taker has the ability to cover the appropriate ranges, for example of formality, purpose or length. Since some topics will appeal to individuals differently, different topics should ideally be included, with choices offered within tasks.

Older children and teenagers can benefit from having a central theme running through the tasks, while younger children may not see the 'wholeness', and may be better served by a 'fresh start' in each task. It should be pointed out that whether the task 'genre' is electronic (e.g. an email) or traditional (e.g. a letter), either can be done on paper or on computer for the purpose of the test.

It should be emphasized that the more young learners engage with the task, the more likely they are to perform at their best. It can be motivating and helpful to give or simulate an authentic reason for the writing. If a piece of writing is to be used in a school newspaper, on a class wall chart or a class blog, or if it is to be written to or by a person in a real or imaginary context that is meaningful, the pupil will see more point in the writing, and have a better idea of what is expected.

Younger Children: Aged 5/6 to 8/9 Years (Approaching A1-A2)

At least at the lower end of this age group, there will be children who can barely write, even in their L1, and provision must be made for this in testing. Below A1, children may only be able to copy words. Around A1, they will be able to write some very familiar words and phrases, gradually linking these into very simple sentences, following a pattern, or using them to fill gaps in simple texts. At around A2 they will be able to write a series of simple sentences. Their vocabulary and concepts will be largely concrete and very familiar. The range of text types they can produce will be limited, but can include lists, labels, charts, as well as simple letters, emails and postcards to friends. The children can be asked to describe people, things, places, likes and dislikes, and, gradually, events (as simple narratives).

The challenge posed by a task is largely dependent on the degree of support and the length of the text expected in the response. Around lower A1, writing the names of things may be done with or without a set of words to choose and copy from. This can include labelling things in a picture and matching things, for example, weekdays and weather, as shown in Figure 6.2 below.

Once children are able to write words independently, they can be given freer naming tasks; for example, if using a basic picture of a classroom, farm, house, or anything they are culturally familiar with, they can be asked to write what they see. This can be in the form of listing or more free writing, for example linking with *and,* and having the chance to expand a little on what they see, for example *I can see a man with a dog.* They can be asked to list things they like, for example, kinds of food, or animals, and things they do at school or in their free time. All these activities can be done

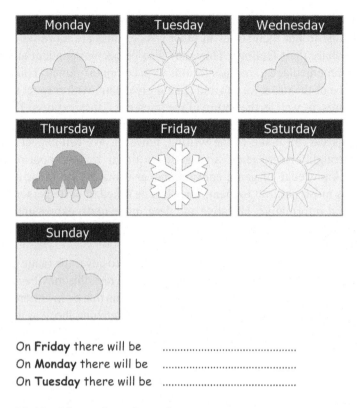

On **Friday** there will be   ....

On **Monday** there will be   ....

On **Tuesday** there will be   ....

Figure 6.2: Matching and copying task

on paper or computer. There can be a place here for using spoken input, i.e. the children hear a word or phrase spoken aloud, and have to write it down. In all of these tasks, the role of spelling can be an issue, and whoever makes/ gives the test needs to consider the extent to which an answer is considered 'wrong' if it is misspelt. At this stage, children need to be encouraged simply to venture to write, and so as a rule should not be penalized for misspelling, unless the test is specifically targeting spelling. If a set of criteria such as those shown here is used, the spelling will be noted as one dimension of the assessment profile.

Older Children: Aged 8/9 to 12/13 Years (A1-B1)

At this stage, children's writing does not only reflect their development in language proficiency, possibly moving towards level B1, but also the changes they go through in other respects. They have started to widen their knowledge of the world beyond their immediate personal experience, are generally more taken up with their peers and what interests them, are better able to put themselves in other's shoes, and are more willing and able to share their feelings. They may also be becoming adept at writing in different media, e.g. in class forums or in computer games. This widens the scope of the tasks we can and should give them, with respect to topics and genres, as well as the nature of the 'messages' they express. The 'ceiling' of level B1 defined here as appropriate for this age group, limits the demands we can make of the writing, however. We can expect them to write straightforward texts, arranged in a linear way, without requiring special knowledge of genre conventions, or using a style other than that which is most 'natural' to them. They can be asked to write personal messages and informative, narrative and descriptive texts, expressing wishes or views, but not engaging in more than the simplest form of arguments or persuasion.

A test for children in this age group will have to cover the range of levels likely to be present in the group. In a large-scale test, this may be all levels from A1 to B1, and therefore should include items that even children at the lowest level could manage, with some items stretching those at the upper end of the scale.

At around A1 to A2, tasks can be similar to those suggested for younger children, but adapted to their maturity/range of interests and to the different text types (genres and media) they are likely to write in. Tasks eliciting single words or phrases can be picture-based, but care should be taken not to make these seem babyish. Pictures can be more dynamic than for the younger children, depicting actions and even emotions. Humour can be used, for example showing a young person's untidy bedroom or depicting everyday things in crazy contexts.

As children reach A2, they can produce texts on topics of their own interest, e.g. simple descriptions of sports or music heroes. They can write emails to people they admire, or postcards from places they know about or are given input on, preferably from exciting places. Many children write text messages (SMS) and blogs on topics of their own interest, and some even have websites, so these can be simulated in test situations where this is appropriate. If the text is linked to reading activities, the children can put themselves in the role of people they have read about. In the case of *The Stolen Elephant* (Hasselgreen 2000), referred to earlier, one of the written tasks was to make a diary entry for a leading character (boy) in the story, who had, at one stage, suspected his own older brother of being the elephant thief. The entries written by the children contained a mix of feelings, including relief at solving the mystery and claiming the reward, but also guilt at the boy's own suspicion of his brother.

To demonstrate their ability as B1 is approached, the children can be asked to write longer, more complex texts, such as a story. In *The Stolen Elephant,* one of the writing tasks was a letter from the other main character telling the story of the whole adventure to her penfriend. Similarly, in a 7th grade Norwegian National Test of Writing (2004) https://www.regjeringen.no/no/dokumenter/nasjonale-prover-og-gjennomforing-varen-/id109339/), one of the task choices was: 'Write a story, 3 or 4 paragraphs, with the title "The Treasure Chest". Start with the sentence: *One day my friend and I found an old map in a bottle on the beach*'. Alternatives to this task included a story based on a single picture, and another on a cartoon series. These tasks gave children the choice either to use their imaginations, or to follow a plot given in pictures. These can be attempted in a simple way by children from around level A2, while those around B1 are given the scope to show how they can structure and link longer pieces of text, in a linear way, and include various story features, such as dialogues, expression of feelings and a range of tenses.

Teenagers: Aged 12/13 to 17 Years (A1-B2) (Potentially C1)

During the teenage years, the abilities to argue, putting points for and against, and to persuade others to see our point of view gradually develop. The linguistic agility to do these skilfully through syntax and the use of adverbial conjuncts, such as *however* and *although,* requires a near adult maturity, as indicated in Chapter 1. For a teenager to show that s/he is around level B2 and above, s/he has to demonstrate the ability to do this kind of argumentative/persuasive writing, to adapt the style to some extent to the situation or reader, and to structure a piece of writing in a way appropriate to the genre/task. Thus, for older teenagers at least, tasks should be given to elicit evidence of all these abilities, while younger teenagers, who are not likely to fully reach B2, might at least demonstrate whether they are able to use different levels of formality. Tasks for teenagers who are around level B1 and below should give them the chance to demonstrate what they can do, in ways similar to those described for older children, while taking into account teenagers' greater topic and world knowledge, as well as their familiarity with different genres.

Drew and Sørheim (2009: 88–89) list three main categories of genre, which should be represented in writing in the secondary school context:

1. Creative/expressive (for example narratives, poems, dialogues)
2. Functional (for example letters, e-mails, articles, advertisements, instructions)
3. Argumentative

Tasks making up a test might consist of each of these types for older teenagers, while the argumentative task may be omitted for younger teenagers.

A set of tasks for the younger teenagers might consist of:

- A note to a friend, asking him/her to do something, with key words given (A1-A2).
- A letter containing information to an adult who they don't know well, with prompts given regarding the structure (A2-B1).
- A story, either with a starting or concluding sentence, or with guidance from pictures or some prompts/key words as to what points to cover (A2-B1).

For the older teenagers, all three genre types could be present, and a test may, for example, consist of:

- An email to classmates, informing them of an event and instructing them to contribute, with prompts given (A1-A2).
- An article/essay/ narrative on a topic chosen from several, drawing on the world knowledge expected at this age (B1 and over).
- A (concise) formal letter to a newspaper editor, arguing for a stance and showing an awareness of other points of view (topic given) (B2 and over).

As discussed earlier, young people nowadays often have more experience in typing written communication, for example SMS, chat, blog or email, than they do in handwritten letters. If delivering a computer-based test, this can be exploited by designing and creating tasks which will elicit the kind of language that the teenagers are expected to demonstrate, at the same time using a format they are likely to be more comfortable with. *Aptis for Teens* uses this principle for its test aimed at ages 13 years and above. An example of a task-set of this kind (see Appendix C.5) is as follows:

A1: Sign up to a website or blog
A2: Give a description of yourself, for example stating your likes and dislikes
B1: Take part in a chat, expressing your opinions in a chat room
B2+: Write an argumentative essay as part of a website competition on a given topic.

A task combination such as this will allow the teenagers to show whether they possess the abilities/knowledge to be assessed, from the lowest levels up to B2 or higher, where rhetorical skills, such as irony can be demonstrated. To assist the teenagers to demonstrate their range in ability across levels, these tasks provide thematic/structural support. All the tasks shown in Appendix C.5, referred to here, are related to the same theme (the *Global friends* website), which runs through the entire writing test, and the tasks logically build on each other, as would be the case when joining a real website or social network. The tasks progressively increase the level of difficulty and the demands made. As Merrill (2006) points out: 'A progression of tasks that are progressively more complex during training with the student performing more and more of the steps to task completion on their own enables them to tune their schema so that when confronted with yet a different or more complex task from the same family they are able to move forward to task completion' (2006: 277).

Conclusion

This chapter began by emphasizing the differences in the nature of reading and writing. While the chapter shared some common features with Chapter 5, on testing reading, notably in its presentation of a model as a basis for describing L2 writing, and its age/CEFR-related analysis of characteristics of tasks, in many ways it took a rather different approach.

A main reason for this difference is the central role of assessment criteria (which principally relate to the *knowledge* component in our writing model). These criteria play a fundamental role in deciding not only how texts are rated but how tasks are designed, since these must elicit evidence of the criteria having been met. For this reason, after a short discussion of *processes* and a brief introduction to *knowledge*, *criteria* were discussed and illustrated in some detail, before we proceeded to consider actual testing, focusing on *tasks*, which were characterized for each of the three age groups in turn, adhering to the relevant ranges of CEFR levels established in Chapter 3.

The issues surrounding the testing of young learners' L2 writing overlap, to a large extent, those involved in testing reading. These include the gradual development of linguistic knowledge and ability, as well as issues connected with literacy, genre and world/topic knowledge, and the need to take interest, familiarity and attention span into account. Younger children may be experimenting with writing in their L1, and copying may be all they can manage in the L2 (and this is an important skill at this stage). While correctness will become an important criterion as children mature, at the youngest stages we may simply need to encourage them to write at all; it may be wise to give help in the form of the teacher writing down words children ask for. And talking and/or reading about a topic in advance of writing can have a very positive effect on writing at any age.

The number of tasks that it is practically possible to offer in a writing test may be smaller than for a reading test. This puts a greater onus on test-makers to ensure that the tasks, in combination, cover a range of variables, such as genre, purpose or formality, so that the test-takers are widely prepared for the test, in the interest of washback. Topics should be chosen with care, with choices offered where possible, to allow young learners to write about what they care about. Imagination may exist in abundance in many children and teenagers, but cannot be taken for granted, and some tasks should be offered which support the test-takers in terms of the content, for example, through illustrations or bullet points.

The tasks may also have to cover a wide range of L2 ability/knowledge levels, and it is important that each of those taking the test will have the opportunity to perform at the level of his/her ability. Evidence of ability, used in assessment, should be based on what the pupil has shown s/he *can* do; in the case of a teenager around level A2, a well-written postcard should be given full credit, and not be eclipsed by a poor performance on a too-difficult formal letter.

To conclude, it is worth reminding ourselves that writing is something young learners do frequently in their everyday lives – sending texts and emails, blogging, chatting and playing digital games. The borderline between writing and speaking is increasingly blurred. At the same time, as part of their literacy development, children and teenagers are expected to produce written language which is quite distinct from the spoken, particularly as they move through the school system. The written messages or stories of younger children may closely reflect the way they talk, being mainly constrained by mechanical problems of how to write. The writing of older children and teenagers on the other hand will normally encompass a wide spectrum with near-oral or informal language at one end and quite highly stylized or formal language at the other.

The next chapter will look at the other side of the productive 'coin', which also spans a wide spectrum, but is distinguished from writing largely due to the conditions under which it is produced: speaking.

7   Testing Speaking

This chapter will cover the testing of speaking, which, to a large extent, also involves listening. Most of our speaking and listening are done together, in spoken interaction. When we speak with people, we 'interactively' listen, collaborating with the speaker to arrive at a mutual understanding of what is being communicated. However, it can be useful to know how effectively learners can communicate as speakers, as well as how well they are able to understand what they hear in the absence of interaction. So, in language testing, it is quite normal to test speaking/spoken interaction and listening comprehension separately. This chapter will therefore focus on the testing of speaking in various degrees of interactiveness, with 'non-collaborative' listening left to the next chapter.

Just as writing, as shown in the previous chapter, can resemble speaking, so can speaking at times resemble writing. Luoma (2004: 13) expresses the difference between spoken-like and written-like language as a continuum, with highly literate language and highly oral language at the extremes. Some speaking, such as formal speeches, may lie nearer the written end of the continuum than forms of writing such as jotted-down notes or online chatting. Young learners, as they approach their teens, will gradually also need to be able to speak in more formal, monological forms, such as oral presentations. The focus here will be mainly, but not exclusively, on speaking as interaction or dialogue.

We will start by presenting a model of L2 speaking, and discuss the strategies and skills, as well as the knowledge involved in speaking, showing how these mutually influence each other, working together to produce *fluency*. This will lead us into a discussion on the criteria for judging speaking, including a summary of the way the CEFR describes the development of the spoken language across levels. This will be followed by a practical consideration of tasks, which will be the main focus in the section on the testing of L2 speaking at different ages.

A Model of L2 Speaking

Bygate (1987) attributes the main difference between spoken interaction and writing as being due to two conditions. The first is the *processing condition*, deriving from the fact that speaking is processed in 'real time', with the words 'being spoken as they are being decided and as they are being understood' (1987:11). The second is the *reciprocracy condition,* which derives from the fact that the activity is reciprocal, with the person whom we are speaking to being present, and able, or even obliged, to take part of the responsibility for our message being communicated, for example, by checking for meaning, or indicating understanding or agreement. Bygate maintains that this condition 'compensates in large part for the limitations that derive from the processing conditions' (1987:12). These two conditions constitute the principal reason for what we say generally being so different from what we write.

The components in the model of L2 speaking that is presented in Figure 7.1 include *tasks, knowledge, strategies/skills, discourse* and *criteria.* The tasks, as in the case of writing, are designed to give the test-taker the chance to show how s/he copes with the challenges of speaking, combining skills and strategies with language knowledge to contribute to a piece of coherent discourse, which is then assessed using specific criteria. The points included under *knowledge* and *strategies/skills* are based largely on what Bygate (1987: 50) includes in his summary of oral knowledge and skills. The features of oral tasks in the model are based on Luoma's (2004) discussion of tasks. Strategies/skills and knowledge will be discussed first, leading into a discussion on assessment criteria, followed by an age-related analysis of tasks.

It is worth noting that 'discourse' is used in this chapter to refer to the spoken text itself. The more abstract use of the term has been employed earlier, for example, in Chapter 1, where 'discourse' in speaking was regarded as equivalent to 'genre' in writing. Here, we will distinguish between these two concepts by referring to the text as 'the discourse', and otherwise referring to 'types of discourse', such as interview or conversation.

Strategies/Skills

The strategies or skills used in spoken interaction are basically those we need to cope with the 'real time' aspect of speaking, with a discourse that is constantly changing. We need to know how to deal with and exploit the fact that there is another person involved and we need ways to overcome problems that may arise, for example, due to our 'gaps' in L2 knowledge. After the initial *planning* of the main content/intention of our message, the *management skills* of *agenda management* and *turn-taking* involve our ability, for example, to initiate, maintain and conclude a conversation or to introduce new topics, and to take, hold or yield the turn. *Negotiation of meaning* involves

Features of the task

☒ Stimulus, including visual support
☒ Context (simulated)
☒ Topic
☒ Purpose
☒ Discourse type – e.g. interview, conversation
☒ Structured or 'open'
☒ Number and roles of speakers
☒ Face to face or other, e.g. online
☒ Timing
☒ Preparation

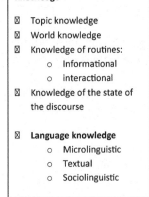

Knowledge

☒ Topic knowledge
☒ World knowledge
☒ Knowledge of routines:
  o Informational
  o interactional
☒ Knowledge of the state of the discourse

☒ **Language knowledge**
  o Microlinguistic
  o Textual
  o Sociolinguistic

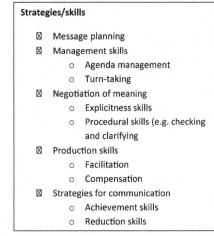

Strategies/skills

☒ Message planning
☒ Management skills
  o Agenda management
  o Turn-taking
☒ Negotiation of meaning
  o Explicitness skills
  o Procedural skills (e.g. checking and clarifying
☒ Production skills
  o Facilitation
  o Compensation
☒ Strategies for communication
  o Achievement skills
  o Reduction skills

The discourse

Criteria for assessing

Figure 7.1: A model of L2 speaking

explicitness skills, i.e. being able to judge just how explicit the message needs to be, which in turn depends on the skill of the co-speaker to signal this. It also requires *procedural skills,* for example, the ability to check and clarify, in order to ensure that the communication is proceeding smoothly.

The *production skills* consist of *facilitation* and *compensation*. Facilitation involves making the language simpler, both to produce and understand. This is brought about by using less complex grammar than in writing, often stringing phrases together with 'and' or 'then'; by using simpler vocabulary, often with generic terms, such as 'a sort of *bag*'; and by using fixed formulaic expressions and cohesive devices such as 'I mean', to keep us going.

Strategies for communication are what we need when our L2 knowledge lets us, or our co-speaker, down. These can be in the form of *achievement skills*, whereby we find another way of saying what we mean, for example, through paraphrasing or *reduction skills,* whereby we sacrifice part of the message, settling for a simpler version.

Knowledge

The knowledge required, apart from topic and world knowledge, is also very specific to speaking. We need a *knowledge of routines*. This may be *informational,* for example, knowing how to relate an event or present a project, or *interactional,* such as knowing how to book an appointment on the telephone. We also need to keep track of what has evolved in the discourse so far.

In the case of spoken interaction, communicative language knowledge, as defined in Chapter 2, is clearly shaped by what has already been described here so far.

Microlinguistic knowledge includes knowledge of the sound systems of the language, in terms of pronunciation and intonation. Pronunciation is important in allowing the listener to clearly 'hear' the message. Intonation, according to Buck (2001: 60), besides conveying attitudes and emotions, actually carries much of the grammatical information in an utterance, while the stress highlights important words. On the other hand, the vocabulary and syntax involved in speaking are relatively basic and uncomplicated. Spoken sentences are frequently incomplete, or even completed by the co-speaker. Phrases and clauses, referred to as *idea units,* are often loosely strung together, in what Luoma (2004:11) refers to as 'spoken grammar'.

It is important, however, not to regard speaking as a simplified form of writing. In fact, it is highly structured, as the turn-taking system testifies. In order to get our message across using a fairly basic set of words, we need other words to signal that these do not carry the precise message; we use expressions like 'pens and things' and a 'kind of soup'. And to signal that we want to check understanding or start a new topic, we need words and phrases such as 'you see' and 'by the way'. These words and phrases are essential to the spoken language, and are what Hasselgreen (2004) refers to as the '*smallwords*' of speaking. In a study of the spoken language of young teenage Norwegians and British native speakers of the same age, Hasselgreen found a clear correlation between the range and frequency of smallwords and 'fluency' as measured in terms of the mean length of turns offset against the number of mid-turn filled pauses (using non-verbal fillers, such as 'erm').

Textual knowledge involves knowing how to achieve flow and cohesion across and within turns (as part of agenda management), as well as how to structure longer stretches of discourse. This involves having a range of cohesive devices at our disposal, as well as the informational and interactional routines referred to above.

Sociolinguistic knowledge involves politeness and *face saving*, whereby we show respect for and acknowledge the feelings of other speakers. We need to know how to soften our views, when to use simple terms rather than say something which may not be understood, and how to express ourselves in a friendly way, for example using *vague language* (Channell 1994), such as 'sort of', rather than sounding like an authority on a subject. This also involves choosing the degree of explicitness. Sociolinguistic knowledge also includes knowing which expressions to use in a particular context; a knowledge of schemata for predictable situations is invaluable for getting by, even at low levels of proficiency.

Thus, Bygate's conditions of speaking can be seen not only to influence the skills/strategies we need, but also the language we need to utilize those skills to communicate acceptably and effectively, thereby achieving *fluency*. Hasselgreen (2004: 134) characterizes *fluency* as what a proficient listener would perceive as spoken at a comfortable pace, coherent and not too broken up.

It can be difficult to distinguish between knowledge and skills/strategies in speaking, as they are mutually dependent, and are used hand-in-hand, in real time. Thus, both tend to be reflected in the criteria for assessment, where references to vocabulary and pronunciation can be found alongside features such as 'keeping going' and 'clearing up misunderstandings'. This will be discussed in some detail in the next section.

Criteria for Judging Speaking

Many of the points made in the previous chapter regarding criteria for writing apply to criteria for assessing speaking. Scales built on criteria may include aspects of the tasks, and the degree to which these were carried out, and the basic messages put across. The skills and knowledge required for spoken communication described above are largely reflected in the elements found in criteria scales for speaking, such as those presented in Luoma (2004). These elements include *pronunciation/intonation, vocabulary, including idiomatic expressions, grammar, fluency, cohesion, turn-taking/holding, handling routine interactions, getting the message across, register and tone* and *comprehension (including actively working with the other speaker to achieve this)*. The elements chosen may depend on the type of task, including the degree to which the speaking is interactive and the roles of the speakers.

Table 7.1: Criteria for Assessing the Spoken Interaction of Older Children (8/9 to 12/13 Years) (Adapted from Hasselgreen and Drew 1999)

Communication BONUS	The pupil has really tried to communicate a message, using whatever language s/he possesses.
Strategies	The pupil avoids using the L1, signalling and trying to clear up problems of understanding or expressing him/herself.
UPPER LEVEL	
Message /tone	The message is put across in a full and interesting way, with an appropriate tone and level of politeness.
Vocabulary grammar	The vocabulary and grammar are sufficient to communicate what the pupil wishes to, in a fairly idiomatic way.
Fluency	The pupil is able to keep going for longer stretches and in turn-taking, without excessive hesitation, at a quite comfortable speed. Uses words like *well, so, I mean* to keep the talk flowing.
Understanding	The pupil understands most of what is said in a clear way.
Pronunciation and intonation	The pronunciation and intonation are generally good enough for the message to be understandable.
MIDDLE LEVEL	
Message /tone	The essential message is put across, with basic politeness.
Vocabulary grammar	The vocabulary and grammar are sufficient to communicate most of what the pupil wishes to.
Fluency	The pupil is able to keep going for longer stretches and in turn-taking, with some hesitation. Uses words like *and, then, I think* to link ideas.
Understanding	The pupil understands most of what is said in a clear way, if the speakers are helpful.
Pronunciation and intonation	The pronunciation and intonation are good enough for most of the message to be understandable, with some repetition.
LOWER LEVEL	
Message /tone	Parts of the essential message are put across, in a neutral tone.
Vocabulary grammar	The vocabulary and grammar are sufficient to communicate the most basic points the pupil wishes to convey.
Fluency	The pupil is able to produce utterances of a few words in length.
Understanding	The pupil understands some messages that are expressed in a very simple way.
Pronunciation and intonation	The pupil can pronounce some basic words in an understandable way.

Table 7.1, which corresponds to the profile scale for writing shown in Table 6.1 (see Chapter 6), exemplifies a scale with three relative levels, suitable for use in the classroom assessment/testing of older children. Here again, bonuses are awarded for *communication*, i.e. daring to use whatever language a child possesses in order to communicate, and *strategies*, such as avoiding the L1, and asking for clarification and rephrasing. The *fluency* descriptors include keeping going for longer stretches, without excessive hesitation, as well as connecting ideas with a range of devices, and using a range of smallwords. It is worth noting that *understanding* is included here, being essential to spoken interaction.

This scale reflects, to a large extent, the elements referred to in the Aptis for Teens scale for assessing speaking (see Appendix B.3), although the Aptis focus is on spoken *production* rather than interaction. Here, reference is made to *pausing, false starts and reformulations*, as well as *cohesive devices and linking of ideas.* Descriptors are provided for pronunciation, as well as for the range/appropriacy of vocabulary and the range/accuracy of grammar. They are also provided for relevance to, and coverage of, the topic.

Like the scale for assessing writing, referred to in Chapter 6, this Aptis scale is linked to the CEFR, with levels divided into two sub-levels. The CEFR (Council of Europe 2001) has several scales which, in combination, shed light on what may be criteria for good speaking at various levels. These are summed up in the scale of *qualitative aspects of spoken language use* (2001: 28–29). Table 7.2 presents the main features of this scale.

Given the basic nature of vocabulary and the uncomplicated syntax required in speaking, it could be argued that B1 in speaking may be within the reach of even the younger children, given the premise that they are only expected to converse on familiar topics. It should also be pointed out that children can master the sound patterns of the L2 at a young age, as has been shown in studies reported by Lightbown and Spada (2006). The CEFR scale for phonological control (Council of Europe 2001:117) for B1 states: *Pronunciation is clearly intelligible even if a foreign accent is sometimes evident and occasional mispronunciations occur.* For B2 the statement reads: *Has acquired a clear, natural, pronunciation and intonation.* In this particular respect, children may even exceed B1. However, as shown in Chapter 3, there are certain expectations which put B1 generally out of the reach of younger children. In the case of speaking, these include the degree of sociolinguistic awareness, which is particularly salient in speaking, and is not highly developed in younger children; the same can be said of their ability to initiate, maintain and close simple conversations. It is probably sensible though, when making criteria scales for children, to make provision for the

Table 7.2: Features of L2 Spoken Interaction Across the Levels A1 to C1 in the CEFR (Council of Europe 2001: 28–29)

	A1	A2	B1	B2	C1
Range	Basic repertoire of words and simple phrases.	Basic learnt patterns, everyday phrases and chunks.	Enough language to get by on familiar topics.	Can give clear descriptions and express viewpoints.	Good command of broad range. Appropriate, unrestricted.
Accuracy	Limited control of a few memorized patterns.	Some simple structures correct. Basic mistakes.	Reasonably accurate repertoire of common routines and patterns.	High degree grammatical control. Errors do not cause misunderstanding. Can self-correct.	High degree grammatical accuracy. Difficult to spot errors.
Fluency	Very short isolated pre-packaged utterances. Much pausing.	Can make self understood in very short utterances. Pauses, false starts, reformulations very evident.	Can keep going comprehensibly. Pausing for lexical–grammatical planning, repair very evident, especially in longer stretches.	Can produce stretches of language at even tempo. Few noticeable long pauses.	Can express self fluently and spontaneously. Smooth flow.
Interaction	Can ask and answer personal questions. Dependent on repetition and repair.	Can answer questions and respond to simple statements. Indicates when following but very limited understanding.	Can initiate, maintain and close simple conversations on familiar topics. Can repeat back to confirm understanding.	Can initiate, maintain and close discourse. Can help a discussion on familiar ground. Mutual confirm and clarify.	Can select suitable phrase for range of functions (smallwords). Skilfully keep floor and relate to other contributions.
Coherence	Very basic linear connectors, e.g., *and, then*.	Can link groups of words with simple connectors.	Can link series of shorter discrete simple elements.	Can use limited number of cohesive devices to link utterances.	Clear, smoothly-flowing, well-structured speech.

possibility that in some respects they may be higher than A2. This is why profiles, rather than single levels, are preferable as a basis for feedback.

As in the case of writing, those using the scale for rating speaking should be trained or given clear guidelines, and in the case of high-stakes testing, inter- and intra-rater reliability should be high. Unlike writing, however, speaking may have to be rated 'live', if recording is not an option. In this case, it can be an advantage to have a very simple version of the scale, which can also be used in classroom observation. An example of this is shown in Hasselgreen (2004: 288). Here, teachers simply have to give a score of 1 to 5, on the following aspects:

- contribution and ability to keep going
- intonation and manner
- pronunciation
- language choices
- language accuracy
- structuring
- listening (understanding)
- listening (clearing up misunderstandings if necessary).

(Hasselgreen 2004: 288)

Testing the L2 Speaking of Different Age Groups

In this section, we first consider some general matters relating to the testing of L2 speaking, before proceeding to discuss features of tasks appropriate to each age group in some detail.

Speaking tests can be very demanding of resources. In contrast to writing, large groups of learners cannot simultaneously take a face-to-face test, with the end products rated later, and this can place heavy demands on time. An online test can overcome some of the time concerns, but is demanding of technical resources. And rating requires that someone listen to the texts in all but the most highly automated tests. As a rule, the more automated the test, the less authentic the interaction will be. Choices have to be made by test-makers, weighing up the degree to which the test tasks are to resemble real-life interactions and the practical, economic and logistic considerations involved in carrying them out.

Luoma (2004) discusses a number of issues which need to be considered in designing speaking test tasks. These are shown in the model of L2 speaking, Figure 7.1, and include: *stimulus* (including visual support), *context, topic, purpose, discourse type (*e.g. interview or conversation), *structured or 'open', number and roles of speakers, face-to-face or other* (e.g.

online), *timing* and *preparation*. We will briefly examine some of these features here, highlighting what is most salient for young learners. The issue of face-to-face or online testing has already been touched upon and will be addressed in the more detailed discussion of tasks below.

McKay (2005) stresses the importance of making tasks motivating and unthreatening for young learners. This can be achieved by giving tasks a game-like purpose, for example, using information gap items, humorous or entertaining pictures and other visual stimuli. Where resources permit, an illustrator is an invaluable asset when making motivating tasks for young learners, particularly for children. For any young learner, an oral test will normally draw on familiar contexts, topics, purposes and interlocutors, reflecting the way language is expected to be used in real-life, which can include the classroom situation as this may be the main arena for L2 use. Some form of role-play in the test tasks can simulate situations outside the classroom, involving a variety of interlocutors, and thereby imposing demands on the tone and politeness of the language used. The discourse types used in the tasks should take into account what is characteristic of the age groups, with conversation being central, and should incorporate a range of functions, such as asking for and giving information, describing, narrating, explaining, getting people to do things, and expressing and exchanging views.

Test tasks can vary in the extent to which they are structured. In online testing, tasks will inevitably be more structured than in face-to-face testing, which allows more flexibility, with the tester adapting to the test-taker's level, needs or willingness to talk. However, a certain amount of structure is necessary to ensure that all test-takers have the same opportunity to demonstrate what they can do. This is particularly important when more than one individual is being tested at a time. Testing in pairs or groups allows for more 'natural' conversation, and more genuine information-gap tasks, but can potentially result in some test-takers dominating the discourse. Hasselgreen (2004) describes an attempt to overcome this in the oral testing in pairs of Norwegian 14 to 15 year-olds. The pupils had paired test booklets, with three complementary tasks that covered a range of discourse types, which ensured that both pupils had the opportunity to participate to an equal degree. A script was provided, which the tester/supervisor, who could in principle be a peer, had to follow. The pupils were paired on the basis of being comfortable together. The script had built-in procedures for the tester to step in, so that if either pupil was unable to carry out part of the tasks, this would not prevent the other pupil from performing.

Regarding preparation for a speaking test, in a recent study conducted by Caudwell and Cooke (2014), the strategies used by 13 to 16 year-old teenagers during planning time for presentations were investigated. It was apparent from the findings that, while the teenagers used the planning time to think about what to talk about, even making some notes, they did not make systematic plans for how to actually carry out the task. This was reflected in the fact that few introduced their presentation with an outline. These findings were contrary to what Wigglesworth (1997) found among adults, who made real use of planning time. This lack of serious planning could be associated with risk-taking, which, according to Morgan (2013), is a characteristic of teenage development.

Younger Children: Aged 5/6 to 8/9 years (Approaching A1-A2, or Higher in Some Respects)

At the lowest levels, tasks for younger children may involve no more than recognizing and saying the names of some very familiar objects, or asking and answering some very basic personal questions. The conversations can be fun and unthreatening if a puppet is used, who may tell some basic facts about him/herself and ask the pupil corresponding questions. Another approach is to simply ask the children to point to objects or name them. Tasks can be given a game-like quality using information gaps, for example where children have to 'guess' the objects, by feeling them in a bag. Working in pairs, the children can name things in similar pictures, and try to work out which things both have, for example, by putting a red dot on common features. The game may involve finding out how many things they have in common. The children will gradually be able to describe objects simply and can be given picture sets, for example of monsters, where each child describes one, with the other having to spot the right monster.

As the children approach A2, they will be able to use and understand longer stretches of speech, and can do picture tasks requiring more detailed descriptions. Pictures of ordinary places, such as rooms, town centres or even buses, can be made much more entertaining and motivating if they have some 'crazy' content. Pictures or charts with days or times marked can be used for describing and comparing daily or weekly routines. The children can be given simple role-plays, such as making shopping lists for an event and acting out shopping for the goods. It has already been suggested here that some children may be at a level higher than A2 in speaking, in some respects. With communicative tasks of the types suggested here, children will perform at their own level, and provision for this should be made in any criteria used to assess their performance.

Older Children: Aged 8/9 to 12/13 Years (A1-B1+)

Older children around A1 will be able to carry out the simple tasks described above, but using pictures more suitable for their age, and asking and answering personal questions relating to themselves or a fictional or factual character.

From around A2, they can carry out picture tasks requiring more detailed descriptions of things and events. For instance, the children can each receive a small set of postcards to describe, to see which cards they have in common. A calendar with events marked can be used in pairs, trying to find a time when they are both free. Role-plays of simple routines, such as ordering food from a menu, can be used.

As the children approach B1, they will be able to give and act on simple instructions and offer explanations. They will be able to recount an event or tell a story based on pictures or other prompts, using a range of tenses. They can be asked to give each other simple jobs, such as fetching something they need, and explaining where it can be found, using picture prompts; this requires some collaboration to ensure mutual understanding, as well as some basic politeness expressions. To demonstrate that the children can keep going in longer turns, as well as short exchanges, mini-presentations on a prepared topic of interest can be given.

Teenagers: Aged 12/13 to 17 Years (A1-B2) (Potentially C1)

Tasks for teenagers should give them a chance to demonstrate a range of knowledge and skills, including the extent to which they can achieve fluency in short and long turns, use a range of common routines, express and exchange viewpoints, negotiate with other speakers to achieve understanding, even in the face of language gaps, and adapt their speech to the situation. Tasks which attempt to elicit this range of skills and knowledge can be illustrated by a face-to-face paired test for Norwegian 14 to 15 year-olds (Hasselgreen 2004: 268–73), consisting of three tasks. The first task, based on a picture story on the theme of teenage loneliness, required that each pupil described one of their pictures, and they jointly pieced together the story, including a consideration of how the characters might feel. This led into a structured discussion on the theme. The second task involved giving detailed instructions so that the partner could carry out a job, such as a Saturday gardening job, or feeding and exercising a puppy. They had to explain what to do on the basis of picture prompts, where it was highly unlikely that both speakers would know all the vocabulary involved. They had to actively negotiate their way to a mutual understanding of the job. The third task involved semi-role-plays, in situations that involved dealing with unknown adults, face-to-face or by telephone. The pupil in the adult role read out his/her side of the dialogue, while his/her partner was told what to 'do' in the dialogue, but had to work out how to express it. Hasselgreen (2004) reports a study using a sample of pupils, both English native speakers and Norwegians, who carried out such a task, involving buying and trying on shoes. As part of the dialogue, the pupil was told to tell the shop assistant that the shoes were too small. The group of native speaker teenagers virtually all said 'they're *a bit* (too) small'. Only one of the Norwegians used this 'softener'; the remaining nine bluntly said 'they're too small', illustrating the importance of vague language to the tone of the speech (Hasselgreen 2004: 212).

Teenagers may be at B2 or even C1, and yet may struggle to demonstrate their level in an oral test situation. Their lack of skill in 'small talk' or sidetracking can lead to repetitiveness or even silences. They are sometimes ill at ease with an adult, and in this respect, computer-based testing can be advantageous; however, this is generally less truly interactive than face-to-face testing, where paired tests, such as the one described above, can exploit the fact that teenagers have been found to talk most easily to each other.

It is important for this age group to be given tasks that are realistic, and to ensure that the test-takers speak as much as possible. While researching the adaptation of long-turn speaking tasks for use with teenagers (13 to 15 years), Caudwell (2015) found that they responded well to tasks that have been personalized and those which provide more support to reduce the cognitive adapting of load. The Aptis long-turn speaking task for adults, consisting of three questions on the same topic, which build on each other (Appendix C.6), proved more difficult for teenagers than anticipated, for two reasons. The first was related to the more abstract and unfamiliar nature of the questions, making them too difficult to answer, and the second derived from the fact that the questions were related to each other. This produced repetitive responses, as the candidates had a tendency to answer all three questions very quickly, then found themselves unable to develop their answer further, other than by repeating what had been said. This was not considered an indication that they were at a lower level of English than the adults, but rather that the task was not suited to supporting teenagers in showcasing their English skills.

To reduce the cognitive load, a new task was designed with more support, both pictorial and written. Additionally, the individual questions were replaced by a task-type that this age group are likely to face at school: a poster presentation. As can be seen in Appendix C.7 (Aptis for Teens B.2 Speaking), the rubric was longer with more explicit instructions, detailing the kind of performance expected of the candidates. The task was contextualized/personalized, by stating that the candidate had made the poster him/herself. This seemingly small change had a significant effect on performances. Candidates often made reference to the poster as their own creation, for example, explaining their choices. This helped them to sustain their presentation, adding detail, and most notably, often speaking as if addressing an audience, despite the fact that the test was computerized. Further functional analysis, based on O'Sullivan, Saville and Weir (2002), revealed that the new task elicited a wider range of functions from the candidates than did the adult task, suggesting that candidates had the opportunity to better demonstrate their speaking skills (Caudwell 2014).

The above study also investigated the use of pictures, and found indications that teenagers had a tendency to get over-involved in the picture, forgetting to answer the question and instead focusing on minutiae within the picture, listing all its features. Bearing that in mind, it is best when developing speaking tasks for this age group to, firstly, decide whether a picture is necessary; if it is only 'window-dressing', it could be distracting for the test-taker. Secondly, it must be decided whether the picture is to be described in detail or used to convey an idea or a theme only. This has implications for the level of detail and items in the picture or illustration chosen. Regardless, pictures need to be clear so that the candidate can see what is depicted and does not waste time trying to work this out. Pictures must also be relevant and appropriate for the target test-takers.

Conclusion

This chapter has presented the testing of speaking, first in terms of general issues and then in relation to a model of L2 speaking, the components of which were discussed, leading into a consideration of the criteria for assessment. Finally, task characteristics for each of the three age groups were presented in turn, bearing in mind the range of CEFR levels considered salient.

Many issues concerning the testing of speaking are similar to those identified in the conclusions to the previous two chapters, being related to the development of children and teenagers, as this is manifested in language ability and world knowledge. However, there are some specific issues related to the testing of young learners which concern not only L2 speaking but also its testing.

The speaking of young learners in an L2 is, to some extent, subject to fewer restraints than reading or writing. Literacy, which cannot be taken for granted, especially in the case of the youngest children, is not a prerequisite for learning to speak in the L2. Moreover, the youngest learners are apparently not as disadvantaged in certain aspects of speaking, notably connected to the sounds of the L2, as they are, for instance, in the case of spelling. It is also the case that the most common discourse type for spoken interaction is conversation, which younger children have been shown to be quite adept at. It was noted in the discussion of CEFR levels (see the section 'Criteria for Judging Speaking') that in several respects, level B1 in speaking may be within the reach of the youngest children, due to the more basic vocabulary and less complicated syntax of the spoken language, even though A2 proved a more realistic upper level generally, across skills, for this group.

However, while speaking itself seems to pose fewer problems, at least for the youngest learners, the testing of it is far from straightforward. A face-to-face speaking test requires that children are given undivided attention, alone or in very small groups, which can prove logistically difficult for a teacher coping with a large class of children. In more formal or external test situations, the presence of an unfamiliar tester can unnerve children and even teenagers to a degree which can seriously affect performance. Computerized testing can help overcome this, but by its nature is less interactive. The design of a speaking test needs to take into account a variety of factors such as if and how to pair test-takers, the kind of input raters should be allowed to give, and how to keep the tasks 'on track', as well as how truly interactive we want the test to be.

By implication, this chapter has incorporated collaborative listening, which is an important part of spoken interaction. In the next chapter we turn to the testing of listening which takes place in the absence of interaction: non-collaborative listening.

8   Testing Listening

This chapter discusses 'non-collaborative listening', where the listener is not in dialogue with the speaker. We do this kind of listening when we listen to the radio or watch TV, hear an announcement, or even overhear other people talking. For testing purposes, the 'text' is usually recorded and played, for example, from a CD or video or accessed online. The way we listen has much in common with the way we read, and the testing of the two is similar in many ways. However, the knowledge involved in following and understanding the spoken language is rather different from the written, as we have seen above. This chapter will build on what has been presented on testing the spoken language in the previous chapter, while it will be structured in a similar way to Chapter 5, on testing reading. Some general issues will be discussed, before presenting a model of listening, followed by a practical consideration of the testing of L2 listening, taking each age group in turn. Some aspects of testing listening will overlap with the testing of reading and speaking; some reference will be made to these, but only those aspects which are particular to listening will be examined in detail.

Listening: Some General Issues

Non-collaborative listening in the L2 shares many features with L2 reading, both of these skills being 'receptive'. In both cases, we try to construct some meaning from a 'text', using what language knowledge we possess. We also bring to the task our knowledge of the topic and our experience of the world, as well as any expectations we have of what the text will be about, often based on the context in which it occurs. The meaning we construct in either reading or listening can be based on a small part of a text or a whole long complex one. The intended meaning may be literal, or it may go beyond what is explicitly stated in the text.

However, there are some major differences which make listening quite special. Just as in speaking, listening requires real-time processing. We cannot go back for a 're-take', or spend time searching for key words, which may be blended into other words, highlighting the need for the training of listening strategies. While we are generally in control of the speed at which we read, in listening, the speech rate is out of our hands. We are also at the mercy of the speaker for the clarity of the speech. On the other hand, speakers will generally want to be understood, and will actively use intonation and pausing to clarify the 'grammar' of the speech. They will highlight important words through stress, and may signal how the parts of the text relate to each other, for example, through smallwords, such as *so* or *anyway*. They will often use the routines and expressions typically associated with the particular speech situation. The more knowledge of the spoken language (as described in the previous chapter) a listener has, the easier the task of listening. There is a clear case for testing L2 listening. While testing reading may be a less resource-demanding way of testing the understanding of the L2, listening and reading are quite different processes, requiring different skills and knowledge. It has also to be remembered that, in the case of the youngest learners, and even some of the older ones, literacy will be lagging behind what can be understood orally, and in these cases, listening tests may be the only accurate way of finding out what learners understand in the L2.

In the testing of listening, as in the case of reading, isolating individual sub-skills, or strategies, can be fraught with difficulty (Buck 2001: 132). We cannot predict which strategies a learner might apply in confronting a particular test item, to reach an understanding of what they hear, but as in the case of reading, we can try to create tests that are likely to activate a variety of strategies. Moreover, a number of factors can be identified and controlled which affect difficulty in listening comprehension. These concern both the text and the task, which must be considered together in estimating the difficulty of a test item. Buck (2001: 149–50) has identified features of the text affecting difficulty as including:

- Linguistic properties, such as speech rate, degree of pausing, familiarity of pronunciation and naturalness of intonation, commonness of vocabulary and degree of grammatical complexity, as well as the 'linearness' of idea units.
- Explicitness of ideas.
- Straightforwardness/predictability of organization.
- Content – familiarity, concreteness and degree of complexity (e.g. number of elements and stability in the way they relate to each other).

However, a text does not in itself contain an inherent level of difficulty. It is what we have to do with it that defines the difficulty. Buck (2001: 151) identifies the following features of tasks which affect difficulty:

- amount of information to be processed – less is easier than more
- location of the information to be processed – information in one part of the text is easier to process than if this is scattered around the text
- recalling exact content is easier than summarizing or extracting the gist
- selecting fact is easier than separating fact from opinion
- finding information relevant to the main theme is easier than finding less relevant information
- giving an immediate response is easier than responding after a time interval.

The formats of test items for listening have much in common with those used in testing reading (see Chapter 5). But if the test is to be a valid test of listening only (i.e. not integrated with other skills such as reading), then the use of written tasks and responses should be kept to a minimum. Pictures are ideally suited to items testing literal meaning, for example, through matching words or longer stretches of language to pictures. Objects can be dragged in computerized tests and drawn in paper tests. Diagrams, tables, maps and charts can also reduce the amount of written text in an item, requiring transfer of information. To test comprehension beyond the literal meaning, it is normally necessary to use some written text however, in the form of multiple-choice or open-response answers, which can, in principle, be written in the L1. These are best used when the test-takers' basic literacy is not in doubt, and thus should be avoided to a large extent with younger children.

Another issue regarding the format of listening tests is the question of how often a text should be heard. Particularly in the case of younger learners, who may be easily distracted, it is important that salient information be imparted more than once. This can be done by repeating chunks of the text, as appropriate to the individual task. However, this can slow down and even break up the discourse, particularly if it occurs as part of an ongoing episode. Ways of overcoming this include producing a dialogue that incorporates each salient bit of information twice, for example, by a parent dictating a shopping list with a child checking it over, or even through rephrasing, so that a semantically related clue is built in, to guide the listener to the answer.

It can be useful and informative to build into a listening test some items which test whether or not children can make the connection between the written and spoken forms of common words. In the case of younger children, a group of words (such as *chair, you, three* and *moon*) can be presented, on screen or in a chart, with the child having to identify words they hear. For older children, lists of words can be shown or short written texts

with gaps, while a dialogue or monologue is played, and the task is to identify or write in the relevant words. These item types combine the testing of
both listening and reading/writing, but target a very important skill in young
learners: matching the words they hear with their written forms.

The discussion in Chapter 5 about scoring/interpreting scores on reading
applies to testing listening, and will not be dealt with further here.

A Model of L2 Listening

We have developed a model of L2 listening, based on the above discussion,
combined with the work of Field (2013a and 2013b), as well as information
in Chapter 7. Figure 13 shows the model, with its four basic parts pertaining
to: task, knowledge, processing and text/discourse.

The model will be interpreted here in the context of a person doing a test
item, which can be considered as an oral text plus any other input, such as
a picture, with a task to be carried out which demands some kind of knowledge and some level of processing of what is heard. Features of the text
and task which cause difficulty have been discussed above. The knowledge
required for listening is basically the same as that presented in the model
of speaking (Figure 8.1), which includes both speaking and collaborative
listening.

However, the processes involved in non-collaborative listening, without a helpful co-speaker, are quite different, and as in the reading model,
are described here as a series of levels. The first level involves hearing and
recognizing the sounds, while the next level, lexical searching, relates these
sounds to words in the language we know. This is quite demanding, as
boundaries between spoken words are not always clear, and what we hear
may not perfectly match the way we perceive a word to be pronounced. At
the third level, parsing, we use our grammatical knowledge to comprehend
how the words work together to make meaning in a clause or idea unit. This
brings us to the fourth level of constructing a meaning of what we hear, if
necessary employing inferencing to arrive at the intended meaning. Gradually, at the highest level we have a representation of the whole discourse.

Testing the L2 Listening of Different Age Groups

CEFR Levels

Based on the self-assessment grid (Council of Europe 2001: 26–27) and the
scale for overall listening comprehension (2001: 66), the levels for listening
can be briefly summed up as:

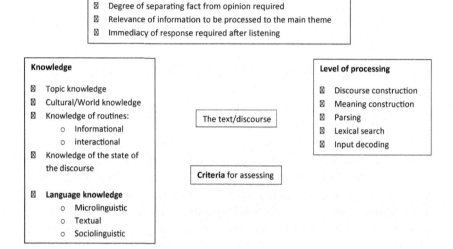

Figure 8.1: A model of L2 listening

- A1: Can understand highly familiar words or phrases; dependent on very slow, carefully articulated speech with long pauses to assimilate meaning.
- A2: Can understand familiar words or phrases; can understand main points in short, clear, simple messages; dependent on slow and clearly articulated speech.
- B1: Can understand main points in clear, standard speech on familiar matters; can follow clear, relatively slow speech on less familiar matters.
- B2: Can understand extended speech and complex lines of argument on familiar matters; can follow most speech in standard accent on less familiar matters.
- C1: Can understand extended speech even in unfamiliar accent and when not clearly structured.

What will be demonstrated here is how the components of the model of listening, shown in Figure 13, can be brought together in characterizing test items for the various age groups, taking the CEFR levels into account. As in Chapter 5, level of *processing* will be discussed, and texts and tasks will be described together here, under the heading *test items*. The knowledge required is considered to be that demanded for speaking, described in Chapter 7 (see Criteria for Judging Speaking), so will not be taken up here. It should be noted that a child may be at a slightly higher level on the CEFR for listening than for speaking, and that the above descriptor for B1 would not necessarily be beyond the reach of younger children.

Younger Children: Aged 5/6 to 8/9 Years (Approaching A1-to A2, or Slightly Higher)

Levels of Processing

At around A1, the child will be able to carry out a lexical search and identify very familiar words and phrases, provided they are spoken clearly enough to be 'picked out' of what is heard. At around A2, parsing will be possible, so that the literal meaning of simple utterances and very short exchanges can be constructed. Very simple inferencing may occur on the basis of a number of very clear clues, such as what the weather is like, when a person is describing how wet they have become.

Test Items

The kind of texts used for children around A1 or under will typically consist of very common concrete words or phrases spoken clearly in isolation or within an instruction, such as 'Click on the black dog'. At this stage, a listening test is more or less a vocabulary test. As children approach A2, they can be asked to follow slightly more complex instructions, such as 'Put the box on the table'. They can listen to short descriptions or simple dialogues, for example, between two children or a child and a parent, and identify a picture or object which is relevant to what has been heard in the text. This may involve a single detail of information in the text or a simple overall idea, such as what a person is doing.

Older Children: Aged 8/9 to 12/13 Years (A1-B1)

Levels of Processing

While at the lowest range of the levels for this group, the children may manage little more than word and phrase recognition, those at A2 and over can be expected to parse what they hear and make sense of clauses and idea units. The constructed meaning can involve detail in or entire short texts. Simple inferencing can be carried out, as long as there are fairly explicit clues given, for example, in the tone of voice.

Test Items

At this stage, a variety of spoken text types from a range of situations can be used, with responses based mainly on pictures or other visual sources, with reading and writing being avoided as far as possible. Dialogues can involve a wider range of participants, such as children and unfamiliar adults, in common situations. This can be illustrated by the listening test 'episode' of *The Stolen Elephant* (Hasselgreen 2000), where most of the items include dialogues. One was in a café, where the task was to write the price that each child paid for what they ordered. Another dialogue involved two children laying plans for where they would go to find out more about the elephant theft; the task was to identify the places from a set of pictures. There was also an item involving a shopping list dictated by the boy's mother. An item not involving a dialogue was taken from a local radio interview with a taxi driver who had followed a suspicious van; the task was to trace the van's route on a map. A simpler item consisted of a monologue, with an irate shopkeeper grumbling to himself as he viewed the mess left in his yard by intruders; the task, based on a picture of the yard, was simply to put a cross beside all the objects he mentioned. In most of the items, all the vital information was mentioned twice in a 'natural' way, without direct repetition of the talk. In an open task at the end of the episode, there was a question based on the events so far, and the children were even asked to venture an opinion as to where the elephant was; this was addressed enthusiastically, but was not scored as there was clearly no right answer!

Teenagers: Aged 12/13 to 17 Years (A1-B2) (Potentially C1)

Levels of Processing

The processes involved in listening in this age group range from word recognition at A1/A2 level, through parsing to literal meaning construction and some inferencing around B1, followed by understanding the wholeness of a longer discourse around B2 and beyond.

Test Items

When testing the listening of teenagers at the lower levels at least, it is advisable to keep to familiar topics, such as school life, friends talking about the weekend, or other matters likely to be of interest. However, the range of participants, topic and situations should vary, and discourse types beyond straightforward conversations should be included. Teenagers have a wide variety of interests and usually love finding out about new things, so even an introductory talk about a new gadget, or a short news bulletin on teenage life in a different part of the world can make a suitable text. It is worth remembering that a teenager generally has a shorter attention span than an adult and will not necessarily be able to process the most abstract topics. In fact, even a candidate approaching level C1 may not be equipped to handle all topics.

The Aptis for Teens test, which targets a succession of levels, reflects a development in the tasks as well as the texts. Distractors are not introduced until around A2. At levels A2-B1, only one question per text is given, whereas at higher levels two may be given. Inferencing may also be required, but this focuses solely on information and meaning that can be drawn from within the text. Inferencing involving describing the feeling or attitude of the speaker, for example, expressed through the use of sarcasm, may be cognitively out of reach of younger teenagers, besides involving cultural knowledge, and should therefore be used with caution. Note that it can be quite difficult to achieve authenticity in recorded speech demonstrating attitudes through rhetorical devices such as irony and sarcasm.

Conclusion

This chapter has presented some general issues related to 'non-collaborative' listening in the L2, introducing a model with a similar structure to that of reading. Aspects of testing listening were addressed for each age group using this model as a framework. As the knowledge required for listening was regarded as the same as for speaking, this was not addressed in detail. The processing, on the other hand, is quite different, and more like that of reading, although this has to be carried out in real time, and is at the mercy of the non-collaborative or absent speaker when it comes to such factors as speed, clarity or accent.

The fact that listening shares a language knowledge base with speaking, with its less complex vocabulary and syntax and independence from literacy, coupled with the fact that, in this kind of listening, we are not expected to produce any language, would suggest that listening is the easiest 'skill' to acquire, at least in the early stages. This is borne out by the descriptor for B1 listening shown here, which seems largely within the reach of the younger children.

However, as in the case of speaking, the testing of the listening of young learners is more complex than that of its written counterpart, demanding greater resources and posing a number of potential obstacles to be overcome. Finding or compiling oral texts is just the start. Decisions have to be made as to how to build in pauses and whether to repeat the text or find other ways of ensuring the information is not dependent on a one-off 'grasping', especially with school classes which may be subject to all sorts of interruptions and distractions. Tasks have to be made which test listening validly, without reliance on reading and writing skills. This can involve the use of pictures, particularly for the younger groups. Large-scale testing for young learners typically requires both item banks and picture banks.

Having highlighted, both in this chapter and that on testing speaking, the pitfalls involved in testing the spoken language, it must be emphasized that any testing of young learners which does not include this somewhere is, at best, inadequate and, at worst, harmful. Washback in the school context is powerful, and what is tested can quickly become 'it', at the cost of all else, in the minds of children, parents and teachers. Communicative language testing, the subject of these four chapters, is of little value if it does not cover the primary form of communication: talking to people.

9 Testing Vocabulary and Grammar

The previous four chapters have solely addressed language testing with a communicative focus. All reference to vocabulary and grammar has been made in the context of the assessment of reading, writing, speaking or listening, commonly known as 'the four skills'. However, these references have been frequent. In the discussion on criteria for assessing writing and speaking, both vocabulary and grammar have been included as components, individually or jointly, as illustrated by the 'profiles' presented for writing and speaking in Chapters 6 and 7. In testing reading and listening, we have seen that vocabulary (defined here as both single words and multi-words or chunks, following Read 2000: 21) is virtually all that is tested around level A1. Moreover, the role of grammatical knowledge (here taken to refer to morphology and syntax) has been acknowledged as distinguishing between levels of processing in both reading and listening. The CEFR scales give broad, non-specific descriptions of the type and range of vocabulary and grammar expected to be known or mastered at different levels, and for many testing purposes, this may suffice.

However, we may want to establish particular aspects of our learners' lexical or grammatical knowledge, such as the breadth or depth of their vocabulary, or the extent to which they have mastered basic grammatical forms and meanings. In such situations, a specific test of vocabulary or grammar may be called for. Read's (2000: 9) model of the different approaches to, or dimensions involved in testing vocabulary is shown in Figure 9.1 below. For practical purposes, the essentials of this model will underlie the discussion on general issues relating to testing both vocabulary and grammar. This discussion will be followed by a consideration of issues specific to the testing of vocabulary and grammar in the case of young learners.

Testing Vocabulary and Grammar: Some General Issues

In communicative language testing, the assessment of vocabulary or grammar is fairly firmly rooted in the right-hand side of the model. The testing is *embedded,* in so far as it is a component in the testing of a wider construct, such as reading or speaking. It is *context dependent* with the proviso

Dimensions most often associated with tests specifically of vocabulary (also applicable to grammar)	Dimensions most often associated with 'communicative' language tests
Discrete A measure of vocabulary knowledge or use as an independent construct	**Embedded** A measure of vocabulary which forms part of the assessment of some other, larger construct
Selective A measure in which specific vocabulary items are the focus of the assessment	**Comprehensive** A measure which takes account of the whole vocabulary content of the input material (reading/listening tasks) or the test-taker's response (writing/speaking tasks)
Context independent A vocabulary measure in which the test-taker can produce the expected response without referring to any context	**Context dependent** A vocabulary measure which assesses the test-taker's ability to take account of contextual information in order to produce the expected response

Figure 9.1: Dimensions of vocabulary assessment (from Read 2000: 9)

that there is a significant textual context, which Read (2000: 11) regards as extending beyond a single clause or sentence. The test-taker will have the support of the surrounding text to arrive at the intended meaning of a word or a grammatical form. At the lowest levels, however, items may occur in which the context for interpreting a word or phrase is visual rather than textual.

However, the degree to which the testing of vocabulary or grammar is *comprehensive*, within the communicative approach, can vary. In testing speaking or writing, the assessment will generally be based on the over-all evidence of the test-taker's vocabulary and grammar, often expressed in terms of range/variety, complexity and accuracy. Reading test items, on the other hand, commonly target selected elements of vocabulary or grammar which occur in a text, although even here, the point may be to gauge the general level of the test-takers' competence, rather than an interest in the particular elements selected. Item types for testing selected elements in a reading text are varied. They may include matching a word in the text with a synonym or definition. Gap-filling or 'drop down boxes' in a text may be used, where a lexical or function word or a morphological form has to be supplied. Questions can be posed regarding the referents to pronouns. Alternatively, a number of connecting words, such as *although* and *so,* can removed and written outside the text to be selected and re-inserted in the gaps.

The left-hand side of the model contains the dimensions associated with quite a different kind of testing. Tests specifically measuring vocabulary or grammar are *discrete*, in that they are solely concerned with these constructs, rather than broader ones such as writing ability. They are *selective* in that particular elements of vocabulary or grammar are selected for testing. While the context is usually minimal, the kind of vocabulary or grammar testing typically carried out today is no longer totally *context independent*. Purpura (2004: 4) cites the earlier assessment of grammar through the recital of grammatical rules. Similarly, it was not uncommon to require test-takers to conjugate verb forms until far into the twentieth century, before the communicative approach to language teaching became widespread. What is normally tested today is the *application* of rules in some sort of context, however small this may be, and as such, concerns language in use.

Vocabulary tests can focus on a variety of features of vocabulary knowledge. These may include vocabulary size, such as the test devised by Meara and Jones (1990). Meaning is most typically the focus of vocabulary test items, often requiring words to be matched with definitions, synonyms or antonyms. Items can also involve collocations, selecting words which are commonly associated with each other, such as *bleeding* and *profusely,* or with the context of use. They may involve word grammar, i.e. selecting or creating different forms of a word, such as *compete, competitor, competition*. They may involve hierarchical relationships, such as *fruit* and *banana*. Read (2000: 181) cites a test type he devised based on several of these relationships, in which each item consists of a single word placed outside a box containing eight other words/multi-words – four that are associated with the single word and four that are not. The task is to identify the four associates. An example of such an item for a fairly low level (around A2-B1) might be that shown in Figure 9.2. In this item, the words associating with *find* are *discover, out, look for* and *lost*, which represent quite different types of association.

Find	Down	discover	Out	made
	look for	fallen	Go	lost

Figure 9.2: Test item based on Read's word association method (2000: 181)

Grammar tests can target specific elements of grammar which may be problematic for the learner group, such as the use of *there is* versus *it is*. Techniques employed in this form of testing typically include gap-filling, with or without alternatives and sentence completion or re-writing, for example, transforming the sentence from the active to the passive voice. Some tasks involve making judgments regarding the correctness of items. The focus of an item may be on the form itself, such as in selecting a present tense verb form to match its subject. However, it may also involve the meaning of the grammatical form, such as use of the continuous aspect versus the simple; this can be tested by matching grammatical form with pictures, or by a supplying a brief context.

An issue familiar to those creating grammar tasks is the question not only of which elements to test, but also of whether the acquisition of a particular element corresponds to some 'level' of grammatical knowledge. Research on developmental stages should ideally be able to shed light on this, and in some instances, this can be utilized in assessment, for example, by testing the acquisition of question forms in L2 English, which appears to take place following a fairly predictable sequence (Lightbown and Spada 2006).

However, the application of developmental stages is limited in assessment, as Purpura points out (2004: 32–38). Only a relatively small number of elements have been found to have any agreed order of acquisition, and this can be distorted by the order in which elements are taught, as well as by the L1 of the learners. Moreover, developmental stages can be counterintuitive. What might reasonably be assumed to be acquired early may actually be acquired relatively late. For example, Pienemann and Johnston (1987: 81) found that the -s form of the third person present verb tense (e.g. he goes), which is encountered early and frequently in most courses, has been found to be mastered relatively late, at the fifth of sixth stages in verb formation.

Testing the Vocabulary and Grammar of Young Learners

Thus far, we have presented a brief overview of issues surrounding the testing of vocabulary and grammar. What has not been discussed is how these relate specifically to young learners, particularly regarding which elements of language might be selected for testing, whether embedded or discrete, and which testing methods might appropriate. While it is beyond the scope of the chapter to address this in detail, some points will be made that should be considered when designing such test items. These are largely drawn from the early chapters in this book, as well as Appendix A.

Regarding vocabulary, it has been established that our youngest learner group (up to about 8/9 years) is not able to cope with more abstract vocabulary or concepts of which they have no personal experience. Nor are they able to organize their lexicon according to categories, and their word associations are quite idiosyncratic. A particular child may be more likely to associate *banana* with *car* than with *fruit*. They may not be able to cope with Aristotelian definitions, of the type: *An X is a Y which…* For the youngest group, therefore, the use of pictures in vocabulary testing is a suitable device, both with respect to content and method. In addition, older children and even many teenagers do not have a highly-developed sense of derivational morphology, i.e. the use of affixes, such as *mis-* or *-ability*, and so may struggle with identifying or producing derived word forms.

Teenagers may still be struggling with more abstract vocabulary, and can benefit from support in some task types by providing context. For example, when testing collocations, it is advisable to provide a context in the stem, rather than simply a list of words to match. These two types of item are illustrated in Figure 9.3, examples A and B respectively below.

Example A

(Context in the stem)

He decided to have a _____ shower before going to bed.

a) quick   b) fast   c) speedy

Example B

(No context given)

Match the words that go together

a. quick   1. food

b. fast   2. moon

c. sunny   3. bed

d. honey   4. keeper

e. bunk   5. wash

f. time   6. day

                   7. night

Figure 9.3: Examples of testing collocations

Providing context, as shown in example A, not only gives support to the test-taker but also ensures that vocabulary in use is being tested.

Regarding grammar, it must be remembered that the youngest learners, especially those below level A2, are at a pre-grammatical stage and do not yet have enough grammatical knowledge to analyse the phrases they are familiar with. Even around A2, it is also likely that, while they are able to produce or understand a limited number of simple sentence structures, they may not yet be sufficiently aware of these to independently generate sentences of their own, and any systematic testing of grammar would be inappropriate.

It is also the case that even well into the teenage years, syntactic development is continuing, particularly regarding the use of subordinating conjunctions, such as *although* and *in case*, and adverbial conjuncts such as *however* and *moreover.* And items that require sentences to be transformed from one structure to another require a degree of logical thinking that may not be developed before adolescence.

Age is unquestionably a factor to be considered, both regarding the content and the way we test vocabulary and grammar. It is also important to consider the kind of task types that this age group is usually exposed to when designing tests. Vocabulary and grammar are often practised in class in gap-fill or matching formats. It should be noted that unfamiliar task formats may cause problems for a test-taker, and sample tasks should be practised in advance. Similarly, it can be risky to present young learners with items containing erroneous forms; children in particular absorb what they meet in print, and may not discriminate between a correct and a faulty construction.

Finally, the wording of both item instructions and the item itself is of great significance in testing grammar and vocabulary. A grammar item should not contain vocabulary that may pose a challenge, and vice versa. An instruction should use vocabulary and grammar pitched at a lower level than that targeted by the item, since children and teenagers may otherwise become preoccupied with the instructions rather than completing the task itself. The challenge for the test-taker should be in identifying the correct word or form to use, rather than understanding the task itself.

Conclusion

This chapter has highlighted some of the issues to be considered in the testing of grammar and vocabulary, and it is not intended to be comprehensive. It aims to provide some food for thought in this area, and to act as a springboard for those tackling test design/assessment procedures for the vocabulary and grammar of young learners.

10 Conclusion

This book set out to shed some more light on the assessment of the L2 of young learners. We already knew that young learners were special, but we wanted to look more closely into just how different they are from adults and from each other, as they progress from school-start to near-adulthood. We have been able to draw some conclusions on the impact of this difference on their L2 and its assessment.

By considering cognitive and social developmental issues, and how this development manifests itself in the first language, we have seen how this may be reflected in second or foreign language ability, and the use this language can be put to across a series of ages. This is evident in such features as the range of concepts children and teenagers can put into words and how they mentally organize these, the use they are able to make of syntax and morphology, the topics they can relate to, and the discourse types they can understand or take part in.

We turned to the CEFR (Council of Europe 2001) as a starting point for developing a system for describing L2 development as children and teenagers mature. Allowing for the fact that individuals mature at different rates, age-group categories were established as: young children (roughly 5/6 years to 8/9 years), older children (roughly 8/9 years to 12/13 years) and teenagers (roughly 13 to 17 years). By considering first how the CEFR levels are generally perceived as reachable across age groups, and then analysing the CEFR's own descriptors of levels, we have been able to identify the following rough correspondence between ages and achievable CEFR levels as follows: young children – A2; older children – B1; teenagers – B2, with some exceptional older teenagers being able to reach C1.

It must noted that the borders between CEFR levels are 'fuzzy', and that some of a learner's skills, such as listening, may be at a higher level than others, such as writing. This applies especially, but not exclusively, to younger children, where literacy cannot be taken for granted.

Some questions were posed regarding the extent to which the CEFR adequately covers what young learners are able to do, and whether a child's level, such as B1, is the same as a teenager's or an adult's B1. Neither question could be answered with an unreserved 'yes', and we concluded that more research is needed before the CEFR can be considered entirely suitable for the assessment of the language of young learners.

From Chapter 4, we addressed L2 assessment and established that we would focus on 'testing' as the type of assessment for the remainder of the book, although not to the exclusion of classroom/formative assessment. Principles of both classroom assessment and testing were presented in Chapter 4 on equal footing, and the role of testing in classroom assessment was emphasized.

Chapters 5 to 8 dealt with the testing of the 'four skills', reading, writing, speaing and listening. A theoretical model of each skill was drawn on, and, keeping the CEFR in mind, along with the findings from the earlier chapters on developmental issues, we were able to draw largely practical conclusions about the testing of these skills across age groups. These chapters focused on the ability to use language in communication, which has increasingly come to dominate language testing, while Chapter 9 addressed issues relating to the specific testing of vocabulary and grammar.

Tables 10.1 to 10.4 summarize what we have established about the development of young learners, and the implications of this development for the testing of their L2. The first table provides an overview of the development as young learners progress through childhood and the teenage years, and the general implications for language testing. The remaining three tables consider each age group in turn, identifying characteristics of the group and how these impact on the testing of reading, writing, speaking, listening and vocabulary/grammar.

In the course of this book, we have relied upon many sources, but for examples of tasks, and how these have performed, we have drawn heavily on our own experience with young learners. The writing of this book has been a learning experience, and so, we hope, will be the reading of it.

Table 10.1: Young Learners (5/6 to 17 Years): Cognitive, Social and Language Development and General Implications for Testing

Cognitive, social and language development	General implications for testing
<ul><li>Potential range on CEFR: Approaching A1-B2 (occasionally C1).</li><li>Development of vocabulary, syntax, morphology and figurative language ongoing.</li><li>Literacy lagging behind spoken ability, especially for youngest, but cannot be taken for granted at any age.</li><li>Gradual increase in familiarity with genre/discourse types, but these need to be taught/demonstrated.</li><li>Gradual increase in interest in/ dependence on peer group.</li><li>Complexity of logical thinking and organization of concepts gradually emerging.</li><li>Attention span increasing, but need for engaging subject matter and tasks persists.</li><li>Ability to make links between parts and whole gradually emerging.</li><li>World knowledge increasing from immediate, personal to more distant.</li></ul>	<ul><li>The size and number of items should be limited by the attention span of the group.</li><li>Topics covered should reflect what is likely to be familiar or of interest to the group.</li><li>The range of abilities being tested may be very wide, which should be reflected in test items. Each test-taker should feel they can achieve/answer something.</li><li>The cognitive demands of the tasks should not be an obstacle to performing as anticipated. Support should be given to safeguard against this.</li><li>Pictures can play an integral role in the testing of children, but should be used with caution with teenagers.</li><li>Test rubrics/instructions need to be very clear, with examples, and language pitched rather lower than the language tested in the item.</li><li>Formats should be familiar, or sample tests provided.</li><li>Items should normally only be linked coherently for the teenage group, where this can be an advantage.</li><li>In spoken interactions, consideration should be given to who the individuals are likely to be most comfortable with. A strange adult may not elicit natural interaction.</li><li>An enjoyable item – with an element of game or other real purpose – will always be appreciated, and can elicit the best from the test-taker.</li></ul>

Table 10.2: Younger Children (5/6 to 8/9 Years): Characteristics, and Implications for Testing

Cognitive, social and language characteristics	Implications for testing
<ul><li>CEFR: approaching A1 to A2(+)</li><li>Vocabulary largely limited to concrete concepts, very familiar range. Literal meanings.</li><li>Syntax and morphology restricted. Simple clauses and straightforward linking words.</li><li>Literacy emerging in L1, very limited for some younger children.</li><li>Genres/discourse types limited to basic knowledge, for example of narratives, description and conversation.</li><li>Very dependent on adults. Not well able to see things from others' perspectives.</li><li>Logical reasoning not well developed. Concepts mentally organized in idiosyncratic way.</li><li>Attention span very limited. Fun and games important. Support may be needed in understanding point of/ carrying out tasks.</li><li>Limited ability to get the gist, and to see links between parts.</li><li>Knowledge of world restricted to own personal experiences.</li></ul>	*Reading* Processing is mainly lexical, with some simple parsing. Some familiar words and phrases can be sight-read, in isolation or in short texts with simple clauses. Tasks can include picture/text matching. A game element is helpful and crazy/nonsense angles appreciated (monsters etc.) Familiar concepts, including colours, pets, weather, self. Text structures are linear or from very familiar genres. *Writing* This consists mainly of writing or copying familiar words and phrases, gradually bringing in sentences, preferably with a clear 'real' writing purpose. Own interests can be drawn on. Spelling may not be an issue in assessment at this stage, where encouraging the child to write may be paramount. *Speaking* In spoken interaction, children may be higher than A2 in some respects, e.g. pronunciation/intonation and basic conversation and storytelling. Use of puppets as interlocutor, for example, can make a test more appealing. Tasks can include naming objects or things in pictures and relating facts about self and own interests. Basic role-plays can be used, e.g. shopping. *Listening* A listening test at this stage will mainly involve understanding vocabulary in isolation or short texts, such as a dialogue between child and adult. Item types need to be practised, and pauses built into the test so that children don't fall behind if taped material is used. Written text should be avoided. It can be an advantage, however, to use some items matching very familiar or transparent written words with spoken form, although this is not strictly testing 'listening' exclusively. *Vocabulary and grammar* As vocabulary (words and phrases) is mainly concrete at this stage, it can be tested by matching pictures with written or spoken word forms. Word associations are best avoided. Grammar is not normally tested at this largely pre-grammatical stage.

Table 10.3: Older Children (8/9 to 12/13 Years): Characteristics, and Implications for Testing

Cognitive, social and language characteristics	Implications for testing
• CEFR: A1 to B1 • Vocabulary, rapidly expanding to cover more abstract concepts. Some appreciation of literal and figurative meanings. • Can cope with more complex sentences, with range of linking words. Understanding of basic affixes. • L1 literacy skills should enable quite fluent reading, adjusting for purpose. This cannot be taken for granted however. • Refining basic genres/discourse types. Can give instructions. Less repetitive. • Peers become important. Gradually able to see others' perspectives and collaborate. • Can cope with simple logical problems and definitions of common nouns. Concepts mentally organized in hierarchies. • Attention span increasing. Fun and games remain important. • Starting to form gist of texts, and see 'wholeness' in parts. • World knowledge beyond everyday situations, including relationships and opinions.	*Reading* Both short texts, e.g. linked to pictures, and longer texts, up to about 2-3 paragraphs, can be used. Tasks can include reading for detail, skimming for information, getting the gist of the text, and making links across paragraphs. Easy items can be given even on longer, more complex texts, for example identifying lexical items. Texts can be informative, instructive or entertaining, and can include expressing feelings, in a range of familiar genres. Tasks can require using reasoning, for example to find subtle differences in text content. *Writing* Tasks should cover a range of demands, from short simple texts to longer ones, allowing individuals to show their ability. These texts should not normally build on each other. Children can use a range of familiar genres, e.g. email or narrative. They can draw on their own experience and use imagination, although this cannot be taken for granted, and choices should be built in. *Speaking* In testing spoken interaction, pairs or small groups can make this more genuine, but care must be taken to ensure each child is given maximum chance to perform. Tasks can include information gaps and collaboration, e.g. finding similarities/differences in pictures. Role-plays, for example, ordering food or giving simple instructions can be used, as can prepared mini-presentations. Computer-based testing can minimize problems of pairing and be less daunting than an examiner. *Listening* Listening texts can cover a range of familiar discourse types, with a variety of participants. Tasks will mainly include identifying specific points mentioned in the text, but can include getting the gist or inferencing, provided quite explicit 'clues' are given in the text. Written text should be minimal. As for the younger children, a case can be made for including some items which test matching written and spoken word forms. This can be done through reading or writing. *Vocabulary and grammar* Vocabulary can be tested, for example, through matching words/phrases with pictures or simple definitions. Simple associations can be used, such as hierarchies, synonyms or opposites. Grammar can be tested for both form and meaning, e.g. using matching or gap-filling, but avoiding transposing sentences.

Table 10.4: Teenagers (13 to 17 Years): Characteristics, and Implications for Testing

Cognitive, social and language characteristics	Implications for testing
<ul><li>CEFR: A1 to B2 (C1)</li><li>Vocabulary may include low frequency and abstract words. Idiomatic. Gradual grasp of rhetoric, such as irony, sarcasm and wordplay.</li><li>Syntax and morphology increasingly complex. Can work out meaning of word forms using morphology. Gradual grasp of complex linking words.</li><li>Literacy should gradually enable critical evaluation and sorting of fact from opinion.</li><li>Genres/discourse types dependent on exposure, but potentially include argument, negotiation and persuasion, as well as skilful narration.</li><li>Peers dominate and peer communication is often more successful than with adults.</li><li>Can process large amounts of information and use logic to solve abstract problems. Gradually appreciate complex issues in adult-like way.</li><li>Attention span increased but still need captivating tasks.</li><li>Can perform sets of thematically-linked tasks, if clearly structured.</li><li>World knowledge includes issues from other cultures/eras.</li></ul>	***Reading*** At higher CEFR levels, teenagers can cope with longer, more complex texts, covering a wide but not unlimited range of topics. Tasks can target readers across a range of levels, from testing understanding of literal detail to deciding main points of paragraphs. Genres can include blogs, newspapers and articles, expressing views and solving problems. Short texts can be used, especially for lower levels. ***Writing*** As for older children, writing tasks should cover range of lengths and complexity. These can be thematically linked, and can include information, opinion, argumentation, persuasion and narration. Differing degrees of formality should be demanded to elicit sociolinguistic skills. ***Speaking*** Tasks should allow teenagers to demonstrate a range of skills – using routines, expressing views and negotiating, in dialogue and monologue. Role-play can vary in participants and degrees of politeness required. Teenagers interact best with each other and may 'dry up' in conversation with an unknown adult. They may lack small talk and the 'worldliness' necessary to keep going, so they need structured tasks, such as giving a presentation, rather than just 'talking about something'. Pictures can be used to advantage, but may be distracting if not strictly necessary. ***Listening*** Texts should be based on a wide range of situations and participants. However, attention span is still not at adult level, so texts should be of the type that are likely to have teenage appeal. Questions are best kept to what is fairly clearly communicated; irony and sarcasm may be culturally inaccessible. For learners at lower levels, questions can be given targeting explicit aspects of the text. ***Vocabulary and grammar*** Items testing vocabulary can be based on associations, including collocational and stylistic. Task types can test both meaning and use of words/phrases. Grammar testing – of meaning and use – can be based on quite advanced syntax and morphology, including 'word grammar'. A wide range of linking words may be tested. Sentence transposing can be used at this stage, e.g. converting active to passive voice.

Bibliography

Alderson, J. C. (2000). *Assessing Reading*. Cambridge: Cambridge University Press.

Allington, R. L. (2015). *What Really Matters for Middle School Readers.* New York: Pearson.

Asch, S. E. and Nerlove, H. (1960). The Development of Double-function Terms in Children: An Exploratory Investigation. In B. Kaplan and S. Wapner (eds) *Perspectives in Psychological Theory: Essays in Honour of Heinz Werner*, 47–60. New York: International Universities Press.

Bachman, L. F. and Palmer, A. S. (1996). *Language Testing in Practice*. Oxford: Oxford University Press.

Bachman, L. F. and Palmer, A. S. (2010). *Language Assessment in Practice: Developing Language Assessments and Justifying their Use in the Real World.* Oxford: Oxford University Press.

Bardovi-Harlig, K. and Griffin, R. (2005). L2 Pragmatic Awareness: Evidence from the ESL Classroom. *System* 33(3): 401–15.

Bereiter, C. and Scardamalia, M. (1987). *The Psychology of Written Composition.* Hillsdale, NJ: Lawrence Erlbaum Associates.

Brinton, B. and Fujiki, M. (1984). Development of Topic Manipulation Skills in Discourse. *Journal of Speech and Hearing Research* 7: 350–58.

Buck, G. (2001). *Assessing Listening*. Cambridge: Cambridge University Press.

Bygate, M. (1987). *Speaking.* Oxford: Oxford University Press.

Cameron, L. (2001). *Teaching Languages to Young Learners.* Cambridge: Cambridge University Press.

Canale, M. and Swain, M. (1980). Theoretical Bases of Communicative Approaches to Second Language Teaching and Testing. *Applied Linguistics* 1: 1–43.

Capelli, H. S., Nakagawa, N. and Madden, C. M. (1990). How Children Understand Sarcasm. The Role of Context and Intonation. *Child Development* 61: 1824–841.

Carlisle, J. (2000). Awareness of the Structure and Meaning of Morphologically Complex Words: Impact on Reading. *Applied Psycholinguistics* 9: 247–66.

Carter, R. and McCarthy, M. (2006). *Cambridge Grammar of English*. Cambridge: Cambridge University Press.

Caudwell, G. and Cooke, S. (2014). Planning to Speak. New Directions Conference, Tokyo, Japan.

Caudwell, G. (2014). *Function Analysis Report for Aptis for Teens*. London: British Council.

Caudwell, G. (2015). *Aptis for Teens Technical Report*. London: British Council.

Cekaite, A. (2008). Developing Conversational Skills in a Second Language. In J. Philp, R. Oliver and A. Mackey (eds) *Second Language Acquisition and the Younger Learner: Child's Play?*, 83–104. Amsterdam: Benjamin.

Cekaite, A. (2007). A Child's Development of Interactional Competence in a Swedish L2 Classroom. *The Modern Language Journal* 91(1): 45–62.

Channell, J. (1994). *Vague Language.* Oxford: Oxford University Press.

Choi, I-C., Kim, K. S. and Boo, J. (2003). Comparability of a Paper-based Language Test and a Computer-based Language Test. *Language Testing* 20(3): 295–320.

Chvala, L. (2012). Genre and Situational Features in Oral Exam Tasks in 10th Grade. Developing a Framework for Assessing Writing in Primary School English. In A. Hasselgreen, I. Drew and B. Sørheim (eds) *The Young Language Learner: Research-based Insights into Teaching and Learning*, 233–46. Bergen: Fagbokforlag.

Clarke, S. (2001). *Unlocking Formative Assessment: Practical Strategies for Enhancing Pupils' Learning in the Primary Classroom.* London: Hodder Education.

Clarke, S. (2008). *Active Learning through Formative Assessment.* London: Hodder Education.

Conradi, K., Jang, B. G., Bryant, K., Craft, A. and McKenna, M. C. (2013). Measuring Adolescents' Attitudes toward Reading. *Journal of Adolescent and Adult Literacy* 56(7): 565–76.

Council of Europe (2001). *Common European Framework for Languages: Learning, Teaching and Assessment.* Cambridge: Cambridge University Press.

Crowhurst, M. (1987). Cohesion in Argument and Narration at Three Grade Levels. *Research in the Teaching of English* 21: 185–201.

Crowhurst, M. and Piche, G. L. (1979). Audience and Mode of Discourse Effect on Syntactic Complexity in Writing at Two Grade Levels. *Research in the Teaching of English* 13: 101–109.

Crystal, D. (1997). *The Cambridge Encyclopaedia of Language.* Cambridge: Cambridge University Press.

Davies, A. (1990). *Principles of Language Testing.* Oxford: Blackwell.

Drew, I. and Sørheim, B. (2009). *English Teaching Strategies: Methods for English Teachers of 10–16-Year Olds.* Oslo: Samlaget.

Dorval, B. and Eckerman, C. (1984). Developmental Trends in the Quality of Conversation Achieved by Small Groups of Acquainted Peers. *Monographs of the Society for Research in Child Development* 49.

Douglas, J. D. and Peel, B. (1979). The Development of Metaphor and Proverb Translation in Children Grades 1 Through 7. *Journal of Educational Research* 73: 116–19.

Elen, J. and Clark, R. (eds) (2006). *Handling Complexity in Learning Environments.* Oxford: Elsevier.

Epstein, H. T. (1986). Stages in Human Brain Development. *Developmental Brain Research* 30(1): 114–19.

Evans, M. A. and Gamble, D. L. (1988). Attribute Saliency and Metaphor Interpretation in School-age Children. *Journal of Child Language* 15: 435–49.

Field, J. (2013a). Cognitive Validity. In A. Geranpayeh and L. Taylor (eds) *Examining Listening*, 77–151. Cambridge: Cambridge University Press.

Field, J. (2013b). *Aptis Test of Listening: Draft Report and Recommendations.* Internal Research Report. London: British Council.

Fletcher, P. and Garman, M. (eds) (1986). *Language Acquisition: Studies in First Language Development* (2nd edition). Cambridge: Cambridge University Press.

Gardner, J. (ed.) (2006). *Assessment and Learning.* London: Sage.

Gardner, J., Harlen, W., Hayward, L. and Stobart, G. (eds) (2010). *Developing Teacher Assessment.* Maidenhead: McGraw-Hill Education.

Gebhard, M. and Harman, R. (2011). Reconsidering Genre Theory in K-12 Schools: A Response to School Reforms in the United States. *Journal of Second Language Writing* 20: 45–55.

Geranpayeh, A. and Taylor L. (eds) (2013). *Examining Listening.* Cambridge: Cambridge University Press.

Grellet, F. (1981). *Developing Reading Skills.* Cambridge: Cambridge University Press.

Halliday, M. A. K. (2003). *The Language of Early Childhood.* London: Continuum.

Harlen, W. and Gardner, J. (2010). Assessment to Support Learning. In J. Gardner, W. Harlen, L. Hayward and G. Stobart (eds) *Developing Teacher Assessment.* Maidenhead: McGraw-Hill Education.

Hartas, D. (2011). Families' Social Backgrounds Matter: Socio-economic Factors, Home Learning and Young Children's Language, Literacy and Social Outcomes. *British Educational Journal* 37(6): 893–914.

Hasselgreen, A. (2000). The Assessment of the English Ability of Young Learners in Norwegian Schools: An Innovative Approach. *Language Testing* 17(2): 261–77.

Hasselgreen, A. (2003). *Bergen Can do Project.* Graz: European Centre for Modern Languages.

Hasselgreen, A. (2004). *Testing the Spoken English of Young Norwegians: A Study of Test Validity and the Role of Smallwords in Contributing to Pupils' Fluency.* Cambridge: Cambridge University Press.

Hasselgreen, A. and Drew, I. (1999). Kartlegging av *Kommunikative Kompetanse i Engelsk: Teachers' Handbook.* Oslo: Nasjonalt læremiddelsenter/Utdanningsdirektoratet.

Hasselgreen A., Drew, I. and Sørheim, B. (eds) (2012). *The Young Language Learner: Research-based Insights into Teaching and Learning.* Bergen: Fagbokforlag.

Hasselgreen, A. and Helness, H. (2014). The CEFR and Testing Children's Reading. Presentation at the 11th EALTA Conference, Warwick.

Hasselgreen, A., Kaledaite, V., Maldonado Martin, N. and Pizorn, K (2011). *Assessment of Young Learner Literacy Linked to the Common European Framework of Reference for Languages.* Graz: European Centre for Modern Languages.

Hasselgreen, A. and Moe, E. (2006). Young Learners' Writing and the CEFR: Where Practice Tests Theory. Presentation at the 3rd EALTA Conference, Krakow.

Helness, H. L. (2012). A Comparison of the Study of Vocabulary of 7th and 10th Graders' Scripts from the National Test of Writing in English. In A. Hasselgreen, I. Drew and B. Sørheim (eds) *The Young Language Learner: Research-based Insights into Teaching and Learning,* 145–58. Bergen: Fagbokforlag.

Hoffner, C., Cantor, J. and Badzinski, D. M. (1990). Children's Understanding of Adverbs Denoting Degree of Likelihood. *Journal of Child Language* 17: 217–31.

Hymes, D. (1972). On Communicative Competence. In J. B. Pride and J. Holmes (eds) *Sociolinguistics,* 269–93. Harmondsworth: Penguin.

Jones, T. and Brown, C. (2011). Reading Engagement: A Comparison Between E-books and Traditional Print Books in an Elementary Classroom. *International Journal of Instruction* 4(2): 5–23.

Kamil, M. L., Mosenthal, P. B. and Barr, R. (eds) (2000). *Handbook of Reading Research* 3. Mahwah, NJ: Lawrence Erlbaum Associates.

Kaplan, B. and Wapner, S. (1960). *Perspectives in Psychological Theory: Essays in Honour of Heinz Werner:* New York: International Universities Press.

Karmiloff-Smith, A. (1986). Some Fundamental Aspects of Language Development after Age 5. In P. Fletcher and M. Garman (eds) *Language Acquisition: Studies in First Language Development* (2nd edition), 455–74. Cambridge: Cambridge University Press.

Katz, E. and Brent, S. B. (1986). Understanding Connectives. *Journal of Verbal Learning and Verbal Behaviour* 7: 501–509.

Khalifa, H. and Weir, C. J. (2009). Examining Reading. Research and Practice in Assessing Second Language Reading. *Studies in Language Testing* 29. Cambridge University Press.

Kibler, A. (2011). 'I write it in a way that people can read it': How Teachers and Adolescent L2 Writers Describe Content Area Writing. *Journal of Second Language Writing* 20: 211–26.

Lantolf, J. P. and Poehner, M. E. (2010). Dynamic Assessment in the Classroom: Vygotskian Praxis for Second Language Development. *Language Teaching Research* 15(1): 11–33.

Larson, V. L. and McKinley, N. L. (1998). Characteristics of Adolescents' Conversation: A Longitudinal Study. *Clinical Linguistics and Phonetics* 12: 183–203.

Leadholm, B. J. and Miller, J. F. (1992). *Language Sample Analysis: the Wisconsin Guide.* Madison: Wisconsin Department of Public Instruction.

Lefever, S. C. (2012). Incidental Foreign Language Learning in Young Children. In A. Hasselgreen, I. Drew and B. Sørheim (eds) *The Young Language Learner: Research-based Insights into Teaching and Learning*, 87–100. Bergen: Fagbokforlag.

Lightbown, P. M. and Spada, N. (2006). *How Languages are Learned.* Oxford: Oxford University Press.

Little, D. (2006). The Common European Framework of Reference for Languages: Content, Purpose, Origin, Reception and Impact. *Language Teaching* 39(3): 167–90.

Little, D. (2012). The European Language Portfolio in Whole-school Use. *Innovation in Language Learning and Teaching* 6(3): 275–85.

Little, D. and Erickson, G. (2015). Learner Identity, Learner Agency, and the Assessment of Language Proficiency: Some Reflections Prompted by the Common European Framework of Reference for Languages. *Annual Review of Applied Linguistics* 35: 120–39.

Loban, W. (1976). *Language Development: Kindergarten through Grade 12* (Research Report No. 18). Urbana IL: National Council of English Teachers.

Luoma, S. (2004). *Assessing Speaking.* Cambridge: Cambridge University Press.

Lloyd, P. (1991). Strategies Used to Communicate Route Directions by Telephone: a Comparison of the Performance of 7 year-Olds, 10 Year-Olds, and Adults. *Journal of Child Language* 18: 171–89.

Manger, T., Eikeland, O-J. and Vold, V. (2009). A Web-based National Test of English Reading as a Foreign Language: Does It Test Language Ability, or Computer Competence? *Nordic Journal of Digital Literacy* 4: 143–58.

McKay, P. (2005). *Assessing Young Language Learners.* Cambridge: Cambridge University Press.

Mahony, D. L. (1994). Using Sensitivity to Word Structure to Explain Variance in High School and College Level Reading Ability. *Reading and Writing* 6: 19–44.

Meara, P. and Jones, G. (1990). Eurocentres Vocabulary Size Test. Version E1.1/ K10. Zurich: Eurocentres Learning Service.

Merrill, M. D. (2006). Hypothesized Performance on Complex Tasks as a Function of Scaled Instructional Strategies. In J. Elen and R. Clark (eds) *Handling Complexity in Learning Environments*, 265–82. Oxford: Elsevier.

Messick, S. (1996). Validity and Washback in Language Testing. *Language Testing* 13(3): 241–56.

Morgan, N. (2013). *Blame My Brain. The Amazing Teenage Brain Revealed.* London: Walker Books Ltd.

Moss, P., Girard, B. and Haniford, L. (2006). Validity in Educational Assessment. *Review of Research in Education* 30: 109–162.

Nagy, W. E. and Scott, J. A. (2000). Vocabulary Processes. In M. L. Kamil, P. B. Mosenthal and R. Barr (eds) *Handbook of Reading Research* 3, 269–84. Mahwah, NJ: Lawrence Erlbaum Associates.

Nippold, M. A. (2006). *Later Language Development.* Austin, TX: Pro-ed.

Nippold, M. A., Hesketh, L. J., Duthie, J. K. and Mansfield. T. C. (2005). Conversation versus Expository Discourse: a Study of Syntactic Development in Children, Adolescents and Adults. *Journal of Speech, Language and Hearing Research* 27: 197–205.

Nippold, M. A., Ward-Lonergan, J. M. and Fanning, J. L. (2005). Persuasive Writing in Children, Adolescents, and Adults: a Study of Syntactic, Semantic and Pragmatic Development. *Language, Speech and Hearing Services in Schools* 36: 125–38.

Nikolov, M. and Csapo, B. (2010). The Relationship Between Reading Skills in Early English As a Foreign Language and Hungarian As a First Language. *International Journal of Bilingualism* 14(3): 315–29.

Nunan, D. (ed.) (1987). *Applying Second Language Acquisition Research.* Adelaide: National Curriculum Resource Centre.

Ortmeier-Hooper, C. and Enright, K. A. (2011). Mapping New Territory: Toward an Understanding of Adolescent L2 Writers and Writing in US Contexts. *Journal of Second Language Writing* 20: 167–81.

O'Sullivan, B., Saville, N. and Weir, J. C. (2002). Using Observation Checklists to Validate Speaking-test Tasks. *Language Testing* 19(1): 33–56.

Philp, J. and Duchesne, S. (2008). When the Gate Opens: The Interaction Between Social Goals in Child Second Language Development. In J. Philp, R. Oliver and A. Mackey (eds) *Second Language Acquisition and the Younger Learner: Child's Play?* 83–104. Amsterdam: Benjamin.

Philp, J., Oliver, R. and Mackey, A. (2008). *Second Language Acquisition and the Younger Learner: Child's Play?* Amsterdam: Benjamin.

Piaget, J. (1926). *The Language and Thought of the Child.* New York: Harcourt Brace.

Piche, G. L., Rubin, D. L. and Michlin, M. L. (1978). Age and Social Class in Children's Use of Persuasive Communicative Appeals. *Child Development* 49: 773–80.

Pienemann, M. and Johnston, M. (1987). Factors Influencing the Development of Language Proficiency. In D. Numan (ed.) *Applying Second Language Acquisition Research*, 45–142. Adelaide: National Curriculum Resource Centre.

Pinter, A. (2011). *Children Learning Second Languages.* Basingstoke: Palgrave Macmillan.

Pride, J. B. and Holmes, J. (eds) (1972). *Sociolinguistics.* Harmondsworth: Penguin.

Puckett, M. B. and Black, J. K. (2000). *Authentic Assessment of the Young Child.* Upper-Saddle River, NJ: Prentice-Hall.

Purpura, J. E. (2004). *Assessing Grammar*. Cambridge: Cambridge University Press.

Read, J. (2000). *Assessing Vocabulary*. Cambridge: Cambridge University Press.

Rixon, S. (2013). *Survey of Policy and Practice in Primary English Language Teaching Worldwide*. London: British Council.

Rose, K. R. (2005). On the Effects of Instruction in Second Language Pragmatics. *System* 33(3): 385–99.

Scott, C. M. (1984). Adverbial Connectivity in Conversations of Children 6 to 12. *Journal of Child Language* 11: 423–52.

Selman, R. L., Schorin, M. Z., Stone, C. R. and Phelps, E. (1983). A Naturalistic Study of Children's Understanding. *Developmental Psychology* 19: 82–102.

Smith, F., Hardman, F., Wall, K. and Mroz, M. (2004). Interactive Whole Class Teaching in the National Literacy and Numeracy Strategies. *British Educational Journal* 30(3): 395–411.

Stein, N. L. and Glenn, C. G. (1979). An Analysis of Story Comprehension in Elementary School Children. *New Directions in Discourse Processing* 2: 53–120.

Stobart, G. (2006). The Validity of Formative Assessment. In J. Gardner (ed.) *Assessment and Learning*. London: Sage.

Tahta, S., Wood, M. and Loewenthal, K. (1981). Age Changes in the Ability to Replicate Foreign Pronunciation and Intonation. *Language and Speech* 24(4): 363–72.

Torrance, H. and Pryor, J. (1998). *Investigating Formative Assessment*. Buckingham: Open University Press.

Van Ek, J. A. and Trim, J. L. M. (1993). *Threshold Level 1990.* Strasbourg: Council of Europe.

Van Gelderen, A., Schoonen, R., Stoel, R-D., de Glopper. K. and Hulstijn, J. (2007). Development of Adolescent Reading Comprehension in Language 1 and Language 2: A Longitudinal Analysis of Constituent Components. *Journal of Educational Psychology* 99(3): 477–91.

Van Schooten, E., de Glopper, K. and Stoel, R. (2004). Development of Attitude toward Reading Adolescent Literature and Literary Reading Behavior. *Poetics* 30: 169–94.

Van Steensel, R., Oostdam, R. and van Gelderen, A. (2013). Assessing Reading Comprehension in Adolescent Low Achievers: Subskills Identification and Task Specificity. *Language Testing* 30(1).

Vygotsky, L. S. (1978). Mind in Society: the Development of Higher Psychological Processes. Cambridge, MA: Harvard University Press.

Weigle, S. C. (2002). *Assessing Writing*. Cambridge: Cambridge University Press.

Weir, C. (1993). *Understanding and Developing Language Tests*. London: Prentice-Hall.

White, T. G., Power, M. A. and White, S. (1989). Morphological Analysis: Implications for Teaching and Understanding Vocabulary Growth. *Reading Research Quarterly* 24: 233–65.

Wigglesworth, G. (1997). An Investigation of Planning Time and Proficiency Level on Oral Test Discourse. *Language Testing* 14(1): 85–106.

Wiliam, D. (2011). *Embedded Formative Assessment*. Bloomington: Solution Tree Press.

Websites

AYLLIT Project
http://www.ecml.at/tabid/277/PublicationID/63/Default.aspx

British Council Kids
http://learnenglishkids.britishcouncil.org

British Council Teens
http://learnenglishteens.britishcouncil.org

Cambridge English Tests for Young Learners
https://www.teachers.cambridgeesol.org/ts/exams/younglearnersandforschools

CILT Portfolio
http://www.agtv.vic.edu.au/files/Website%202015/8871-junior-passport.pdf

Council of Europe, Accredited ELPs
http://www.coe.int/t/dg4/education/elp/elp-reg/accredited_models/accredited_elp_2010_EN.asp

DIALANG
http://dialangweb.lancaster.ac.uk

EALTA Guidelines for Good Practice in Language Testing and Assessment
http://www.ealta.eu.org/guidelines.htm

Finnish Basic School Curriculum
http://www.oph.fi/download/47672_core_curricula_basic_education_3.pdf

Finnish Upper Secondary School Curriculum
http://www.oph.fi/english/curricula_and_qualifications/general_upper_secondary_education

New Jersey Bilingual/ESL Education Curriculum
http://www.state.nj.us/education/bilingual/curriculum/

Norwegian Diagnostic Test of English, 3rd Grade/Utdanninsgdirektoratet
http://www.udir.no/Filer/Vurdering/Kartlegging/Kartlegging-GS-Foreldrebrosjyre-2015-NN-BM.pdf

Norwegian National Tests of English
https://pgsc.udir.no/kursweb/content?contentItemId=40429207&marketplaceId=624075&selectedLanguageId=1

Språkperm Norway
http://www.fremmedspraksenteret.no/nor/fremmedspraksenteret/larings-ressurser/den-europeiske-sprakpermen

Swedish National Curriculum, English 4-6 Grade
http://www.skolverket.se/laroplaner-amnen-och-kurser/grundskoleutbildning/grundskola/engelska

Appendices

Appendix A: An Overview of Nippold's Findings on L1 Development at Ages 5, 10, 15 and 25 Years

Table 1: Stages in Lexical Development (Adapted from Nippold 2006: 22–23 and Appendix 16.1)

5 years	Knows the meaning of at least 10,000 different words
10 years	• Knows the meaning of at least 20,000 different words • Knows the psychological meaning of some double-function term, e.g. *bright, hard, cold* • Knows the meaning of some common prefixes and suffixes • Uses morphological analysis and context clues to learn the meanings of unfamiliar words encountered in reading • Names common objects, letters, colours and shapes accurately and quickly • Uses organisational strategies for calling up words from memory • Defines common nouns by using the Aristotelian form
15 years	• Knows the meaning of at least 30,000 different words • Understands how the physical and psychological meanings of double-function terms are related • Continues to gain knowledge of prefixes and suffixes • Gains proficiency in using morphological analysis and context clues to learn the meanings of unfamiliar words encountered in reading • Uses literate vocabulary in formal speaking and writing • Names low frequency objects, actions and abstract items accurately and quickly • Improves the use of systematic strategies for calling up words from memory • Defines abstract nouns by mentioning key features or functions (e.g. envy is when you covet the possessions of another person)
25 years	• Knows the meaning of at least 50,000 different words • Understands the difference between semantically similar adverbs of magnitude (e.g., *severe, considerable*) • Has knowledge of morphology (roots, prefixes, suffixes) that continues to expand • Continues to use morphological analysis and context clues to learn new words • Gains proficiency in using literate vocabulary in formal speaking and writing • Continues to gain speed and accuracy in naming low frequency abstract items • Defines abstract nouns by using the Aristotelian form (e.g., peace is a condition in which people live harmoniously).

Table 2: Stages in the Development of Figurative Language

Age 5	• Understands some common idioms, e.g., *feeling blue* and concrete metaphors • Produces humour by intentionally misnaming things or creating nonsense words
Age 10	• Can understand and explain the meanings of some metaphors that contain concrete nouns, e.g., *the butterfly is a flying rainbow* • Can understand and explain the meanings of common transparent idioms and common proverbs, e.g., *skating on thin ice* • Uses context clues to interpret some opaque idioms, e.g., *paper over the cracks* • Enjoys jokes and riddles based on linguistic ambiguity • Uses both context clues and intonation to understand sarcasm
Age 15	• Can understand and explain the meanings of some metaphors that express abstract concepts, e.g., *jealousy is a green-eyed monster* • Can understand difficult opaque idioms, e.g., *paint the town red,* and some abstract proverbs • Understands and produces slang terms during peer interaction • Uses sarcasm with peers, parents and siblings • Exchanges humorous anecdotes with peers • Explains the humour in jokes and riddles based on linguistic ambiguity • Explains the ambiguity in some commercial advertisement
Age 25	• Explain the meaning of complex psychological metaphors, e.g., *genius is perseverance in action* • Describes detailed mental images of idioms that are well understood • Uses figurative expressions in formal writing, e.g., persuasive, descriptive • Uses both context clues to understand sarcasm in the absence of intonational clues

Table 3: Stages in the Development of Syntactic Attainment

Age 5	• Mean length of utterance = 6+ morphemes in conversation • Produces sentences with relative, adverbial and nominal clauses • Produces compound sentences with coordinating conjunctions, such as *and* • Produces complex sentences with subordinating conjunctions, such as *because*
Age 10	• Mean T-unit length in conversational discourse = 7+ words • Mean T-unit length in expository discourse = 9+ words • Persuasive writing MLU = 11+ words • Uses easier subordinate conjunctions, e.g., *because, before* • Uses easier adverbial conjuncts, e.g., *also, then, so, besides*
Age 15	• Mean T-unit length in conversational discourse = 8+ words • Mean T-unit length in expository discourse = 10+ words • Persuasive writing MLU = 12+ words

	• Uses moderately difficult subordinate conjunctions, e.g., *even though, so that* • Uses moderately difficult adverbial conjuncts, e.g., *furthermore, nevertheless*
Age 25	• Mean T-unit length in conversational discourse = 9+ words • Mean T-unit length in expository discourse = 11+ words • Persuasive writing MLU = 15+ words • Uses difficult subordinate conjunctions, e.g., *provided that, in case* • Uses difficult adverbial conjuncts, e.g., *conversely, similarly, moreover*

Table 4: Stages in the Development of Discourse and Pragmatics

Age 5	• Actively participates in conversations with children and adults • Takes turns and maintains topic of conversation • Asks and answers questions • Shares anecdotes in simple narrative fashion and retells familiar stories
Age 10	• Tells interesting and original stories with multiple subplots • Talks about characters' inner thoughts, feelings, goals and motives • Uses all story grammar elements in narratives • Uses conjunctions across episodes to create cohesive discourse • Engages in perspective-taking with listener when arguing • Adjusts the politeness of requests, using a wide variety of devices, based on age and status of listener • Negotiates with peers to resolve conflicts • Gives specific and clear route finding directions • Shows awareness of listener's potential confusion • Explains rules of game or sport in an accurate but simple way
Age 15	• Better able to converse with peers than unfamiliar adult • Entertains listener though use of humour, exaggeration and drama in conversation and stories • Produces stories with complete episodes and elaborate detail • Engages in collaborative narrative with peers to achieve group solidarity • States advantages to listener as effective persuasive strategy • Creates well-organised, persuasive arguments, and anticipates counter arguments • Shows growth in mutual collaboration to resolve conflicts • Provides clear and detailed explanation of rules of sport or game
Age 25	• Stays on conversational topic for extended period of time, skillfully using topic shading • Produces large number of factually related comments in conversation • Shows advanced perspective taking in all discourse genres • Tells long and complex narratives, often using adjectives of emotion to describe characters' mental states • Shows skilful use of argumentation strategies and counterargument to persuade others • Provides elaborate explanations of game or sport, reflecting growing knowledge base

Appendix B.1: AYLLIT Scale of Descriptors

AYLLIT – Assessment of Young Learner LITeracy

Levels	Overall structure and range of information	Sentence structure and grammatical accuracy	Vocabulary and choice of phrase	Misformed words and punctuation
Above B1	Is able to create quite complicated texts, using effects such as switching tense and interspersing dialogue with ease. The more common linking words are used quite skilfully.	Sentences can contain a wide variety of clause types, with frequent complex clauses. Errors in basic grammar only occur from time to time.	Vocabulary may be very wide, although the range is not generally sufficient to allow stylistic choices to be made.	Misformed words only occur from time to time.
B1	Is able to write texts on themes which do not necessarily draw only on personal experience and where the message has some complication. Common linking words are used.	Is able to create quite long and varied sentences with complex phrases, e.g. adverbials. Basic grammar is more often correct than not.	Vocabulary is generally made up of frequent words and phrases, but this does not seem to restrict the message. Some idiomatic phrases used appropriately.	Most sentences do not contain misformed words, even when the text contains a wide variety and quantity of words.
A2/B1	Is able to make reasonable attempt at texts on familiar themes that are not completely straightforward, including very simple narratives. Clauses are normally linked using connectors, such as *and, then, because, but.*	Sentences contain some longer clauses, and signs are shown of awareness of basic grammar, including a range of tenses.	Vocabulary is made up of very common words, but is able to combine words and phrases to add colour and interest to the message (e.g. using adjectives).	Clear evidence of awareness of some spelling and punctuation rules, but misformed words may occur in most sentences in more independent texts.

Appendix B.1 (continued)

A2	Can write short straightforward coherent texts on very familiar themes. A variety of ideas are presented with some logical linking.	Is able to make simple independent sentences with a limited number of underlying structures.	Vocabulary is made up of very frequent words but has sufficient words and phrases to get across the essentials of the message aspired to.	Some evidence of knowledge of simple punctuation rules, and the independent spelling of very common words.
A1/A2	Can adapt and build onto a few learnt patterns to make a series of short and simple sentences. This may be a short description or set of related facts on a very familiar personal theme.		Can use some words which may resemble L1, but on the whole, the message is recognisable to a reader who does not know the L1. Spelling may be influenced by the sound of the word and mother tongue spelling conventions.
A1	Can write a small number of very familiar or copied words and phrases and very simple (pre-learnt) sentence patterns, usually in an easily recognisable way. The spelling often reflects the sound of the word and mother tongue spelling conventions.		
Approaching A1	Makes an attempt to write some words and phrases, but needs support or modelling to do this correctly.		

Appendix B.2: The Aptis for Teens Scales for Assessing the Writing of Teenagers

Writing Task 2
Areas assessed: task fulfilment / topic relevance, grammatical range & accuracy, punctuation, vocabulary range & accuracy, cohesion.

5 **B1 (or above)**	Likely to be above A2 level. All features of A2 are met.
4 **A2.2**	• On topic. • Uses simple grammatical structures to produce writing at the sentence level. Errors with basic structures common. Errors do not impede understanding of the response. • Mostly accurate punctuation and spelling. • Vocabulary is sufficient to respond to the question(s). • Some attempts at using simple connectors and cohesive devices to link sentences.
3 **A2.1**	• On topic. • Uses simple grammatical structures to produce writing at the sentence level. Errors with basic structures common. Errors impede understanding in parts of the response. • Punctuation and spelling mistakes are noticeable. • Vocabulary is mostly sufficient to respond to the question(s) but inappropriate lexical choices are noticeable. • Response is a list of sentences with no use of connectors or cohesive devices to link sentences.
2 **A1.2**	• Not fully on topic. • Grammatical structure is limited to words and phrases. Errors in basic patterns and simple grammar structures impede understanding. • Little or no use of accurate punctuation. Spelling mistakes common. • Vocabulary is limited to very basic words related to personal information and is not sufficient to respond to the question(s). • No use of cohesion.
1 **A1.1**	• Response limited to a few words or phrases. • Grammar and vocabulary errors so serious and frequent that meaning is unintelligible.
0 **A0**	No meaningful language or all responses are completely off-topic (e.g. memorised script, guessing).

Writing Task 3
Areas assessed: task fulfilment / topic relevance, punctuation, grammatical range & accuracy, vocabulary range & accuracy, cohesion.

5 **B2 (or above)**	Likely to be above the B1 level. All features of B1 are met.
4 **B1.2**	Responses to all **three** questions show the following features: • On topic. • Control of simple grammatical structures. Errors occur when attempting complex structures. • Punctuation and spelling mostly accurate. Errors do not impede understanding. • Vocabulary is sufficient to respond to the questions. • Uses simple cohesive devices to organize responses as a linear sequence of sentences.
3 **B1.1**	Responses to one or **two** questions show the following features: • On topic. • Control of simple grammatical structures. Errors occur when attempting complex structures. • Punctuation and spelling mostly accurate. Errors do not impede understanding. • Vocabulary is sufficient to respond to the questions. • Uses simple cohesive devices to organize responses as a linear sequence of sentences.
2 **A2.2**	Responses to at least **two** questions show the following features: • On topic. • Uses simple grammatical structures to produce writing at the sentence level. Errors with simple structures common and sometimes impede understanding. • Punctuation and spelling mistakes are noticeable. • Vocabulary is not sufficient to respond to the question(s). Inappropriate lexical choices are noticeable and sometimes impede understanding. • Responses are lists of sentences and not organized as cohesive texts.
1 **A2.1**	• Response to **one** question shows the following features: • On topic. • Uses simple grammatical structures to produce writing at the sentence level. Errors with simple structures common and sometimes impede understanding. • Punctuation and spelling mistakes are noticeable. • Vocabulary is not sufficient to respond to the question(s). Inappropriate lexical choices are noticeable and sometimes impede understanding. • Responses are lists of sentences and not organized as cohesive texts.
0	Performance below A2 or no meaningful language or the responses are completely off-topic (e.g. memorised script, guessing).

Writing Task 4
Areas assessed: task fulfilment/topic relevance/providing reasons, explanations and supporting detail; essay structure and paragraphing; grammatical range & accuracy; vocabulary range & accuracy; cohesion.

6 **C2**	Likely to be above C1 level. All features of C1 are met.
5 **C1**	• On topic. Argument is clear and well structured, highlighting and expanding on important points and providing clear explanations and relevant supporting detail. • Paragraphs used appropriately. • Range of complex grammar constructions used accurately. Some minor errors occur but do not impede understanding. • Range of vocabulary used to discuss the topics required by the task. Some awkward usage or slightly inappropriate lexical choices. • A range of cohesive devices used to clearly indicate the links between ideas both within and across paragraphs.
4 **B2.2**	• On topic. Develops an argument in relation to the topic, providing <u>two or more</u> reasons with sufficient explanation and relevant supporting detail. • Paragraphs are used appropriately. • Some complex grammar constructions used accurately. Errors do not lead to misunderstanding. • Sufficient range of vocabulary to discuss the topics required by the task. Inappropriate lexical choices do not lead to misunderstanding. • A limited number of cohesive devices are used to indicate the links between ideas within and across paragraphs.
3 **B2.1**	• On topic. Develops an argument in relation to the topic, providing <u>one</u> reason with sufficient explanation and relevant supporting detail. • Paragraphs are <u>mostly</u> used appropriately. • Some complex grammar constructions used accurately. Errors do not lead to misunderstanding. • Sufficient range of vocabulary to discuss the topics required by the task. Inappropriate lexical choices do not lead to misunderstanding. • A limited number of cohesive devices are used to indicate the links between ideas within and across paragraphs.
2 **B1.2**	• Not fully on topic and/or: • Expresses an opinion and provides <u>two or more reasons</u> but does not provide sufficient explanation or supporting details. • Paragraph structure not used appropriately. • Control of simple grammatical structures. Errors occur when attempting complex structures. • Limitations in vocabulary make it difficult to deal fully with the task. • Uses only simple cohesive devises. Links between ideas are not clearly indicated which places a burden on the reader.

1 B1.1	• Not fully on topic and/or: • Expresses an opinion and provides <u>one reason</u> but does not provide sufficient explanation or supporting detail. • Paragraph structure not used appropriately. • Control of simple grammatical structures. Errors occur when attempting complex structures. • Limitations in vocabulary make it difficult to deal fully with the task. • Uses only simple cohesive devises. Links between ideas are not clearly indicated which places a burden on the reader.
0	Performance not sufficient for B1, or no meaningful language or the responses are completely off-topic (e.g. memorised script, guessing).

Appendix B.3: The Aptis for Teens Scales for Assessing the Speaking of Teenagers

Speaking Task 1
Areas assessed: task fulfilment / topic relevance, grammatical range & accuracy, vocabulary range & accuracy, pronunciation, fluency.

5 B1 (or above)	Likely to be above A2 level. All features of A2 are met.
4 A2.2	Responses to all **three** questions show the following features: • On topic. • Some simple grammatical structures used correctly but basic mistakes systematically occur. • Vocabulary is sufficient to respond to the questions, although inappropriate lexical choices are noticeable. • Mispronunciations are noticeable and frequently place a strain on the listener. • Frequent pausing, false starts and reformulations but meaning is still clear.
3 A2.1	Responses to **two** questions show the following features: • On topic. • Some simple grammatical structures used correctly but basic mistakes systematically occur. • Vocabulary is sufficient to respond to the questions, although inappropriate lexical choices are noticeable. • Mispronunciations are noticeable and frequently place a strain on the listener. • Frequent pausing, false starts and reformulations but meaning is still clear.

2 **A1.2**	Responses to at least <u>**two**</u> questions show the following features: • On topic. • Grammatical structure is limited to words and phrases. Errors in basic patterns and simple grammar structures impede understanding. • Vocabulary is limited to very basic words related to personal information. • Pronunciation is mostly unintelligible except for isolated words. • Frequent pausing, false starts and reformulations impede understanding.
1 **A1.1**	Response to <u>**one**</u> question shows the following features: • On topic. • Grammatical structure is limited to words and phrases. Errors in basic patterns and simple grammar structures impede understanding. • Vocabulary is limited to very basic words related to personal information. • Pronunciation is mostly unintelligible except for isolated words. • Frequent pausing, false starts and reformulations impede understanding.
0 **A0**	No meaningful language or all responses are completely off-topic (e.g. memorised script, guessing).

Speaking Task 2
Areas assessed: task fulfilment / topic relevance, grammatical range & accuracy, vocabulary range & accuracy, pronunciation, fluency and cohesion.

5 **B2 (or above)**	Likely to be above B1 level. All features of B1 are met.
4 **B1.2**	Responses to all <u>**three**</u> questions show the following features: • On topic. • Control of simple grammatical structures. Errors occur when attempting complex structures. • Sufficient range and control of vocabulary for the task. Errors occur when expressing complex thoughts. • Pronunciation is intelligible but inappropriate mispronunciations put an occasional strain on the listener. • Some pausing, false starts and reformulations. • Uses only simple cohesive devices. Links between ideas are not always clearly indicated.
3 **B1.1**	Responses to at least <u>**two**</u> questions show the following features: • On topic. • Control of simple grammatical structures. Errors occur when attempting complex structures. • Sufficient range and control of vocabulary for the task. Errors occur when expressing complex thoughts. • Pronunciation is intelligible but inappropriate mispronunciations put an occasional strain on the listener. • Some pausing, false starts and reformulations. • Uses only simple cohesive devices. Links between ideas are not always clearly indicated.

2 A2.2	Responses to at least **two** questions show the following features: • On topic. • Uses some simple grammatical structures correctly but systematically makes basic mistakes. • Vocabulary will be limited to concrete topics and descriptions. Inappropriate lexical choices for the task are noticeable. • Mispronunciations are noticeable and put a strain on the listener. • Noticeable pausing, false starts and reformulations. • Cohesion between ideas is limited. Responses tend to be a list of points.
1 A2.1	Response to **one** question shows the following features: • On topic. • Uses some simple grammatical structures correctly but systematically makes basic mistakes. • Vocabulary will be limited to concrete topics and descriptions. Inappropriate lexical choices for the task are noticeable. • Mispronunciations are noticeable and put a strain on the listener. • Noticeable pausing, false starts and reformulations. • Cohesion between ideas is limited. Responses tend to be a list of points.
0	Performance below A2, or no meaningful language or the responses are completely off-topic (e.g. memorised script, guessing)

Speaking Task 3
Areas assessed: task fulfilment / topic relevance, grammatical range & accuracy, vocabulary range & accuracy, pronunciation, fluency and cohesion.

5 B2 (or above)	Likely to be above B1 level
4 B1.2	Responses to **both questions** show the following features: • On topic. • Control of simple grammatical structures. Errors occur when attempting complex structures. • Sufficient range and control of vocabulary for the task. Errors occur when expressing complex thoughts. • Pronunciation is intelligible but inappropriate mispronunciations put an occasional strain on the listener. • Some pausing, false starts and reformulations. • Uses only simple cohesive devises. Links between ideas are not always clearly indicated.
3 B1.1	Response to **one question** shows the following features: • On topic. • Control of simple grammatical structures. Errors occur when attempting complex structures. • Sufficient range and control of vocabulary for the task. Errors occur when expressing complex thoughts. • Pronunciation is intelligible but inappropriate mispronunciations put an occasional strain on the listener. • Some pausing, false starts and reformulations.

	• Uses only simple cohesive devises. Links between ideas are not always clearly indicated.
2 **A2.2**	Responses to at least **two** questions show the following features: • On topic. • Uses some simple grammatical structures correctly but systematically makes basic mistakes. • Vocabulary will be limited to concrete topics and descriptions. Inappropriate lexical choices for the task are noticeable. • Mispronunciations are noticeable and put a strain on the listener. • Noticeable pausing, false starts and reformulations. • Cohesion between ideas is limited. Responses tend to be a list of points.
1 **A2.1**	Response to **one** question shows the following features: • On topic. • Uses some simple grammatical structures correctly but systematically makes basic mistakes. • Vocabulary will be limited to concrete topics and descriptions. Inappropriate lexical choices for the task are noticeable. • Mispronunciations are noticeable and put a strain on the listener. • Noticeable pausing, false starts and reformulations. • Cohesion between ideas is limited. Responses tend to be a list of points.
0 **A1 or** **below**	Performance not sufficient for A2, or no meaningful language or the responses are completely off-topic (e.g. memorised script, guessing).

Speaking Task 4
Areas assessed: task fulfilment / topic relevance, grammatical range & accuracy, vocabulary range & accuracy, pronunciation, fluency and cohesion.

6 C2	Likely to be above C1 level
5 C1	• On topic. Presentation is clear and well-structured, highlighting and expanding on important points and providing clear explanations and relevant supporting detail. • Incorporates all of the information points in the poster into the presentation. Highlights and expands on important points, giving reasons in support of or against particular points of view and giving the advantages and disadvantages of various options. • Uses a range of complex grammar constructions accurately. Some minor errors occur but do not impede understanding. • Uses a range of vocabulary to discuss the topic in the poster in his/or own words. Some awkward usage or slightly inappropriate lexical choices. • Pronunciation is clearly intelligible. • Backtracking and reformulations do not fully interrupt the flow of speech. • A range of cohesive devices is used to clearly indicate the links between ideas.

4 B2.2	• On topic. <u>Develops</u> a coherent message.
	• Incorporates <u>most (80%)</u> of the information points in the poster into the presentation. Provides sufficient reasons and supporting information to support opinions, and describes the advantages and disadvantages of various options.
	• Some complex grammar constructions used accurately. Errors do not lead to misunderstanding.
	• Sufficient range of vocabulary to discuss the topic of the poster, and to use synonyms and paraphrase to present some of the information in the poster in his/her own words. When vocabulary is borrowed from the poster, it is used appropriately. Inappropriate lexical choices do not lead to misunderstanding.
	• Pronunciation is intelligible. Mispronunciations do not put a strain on the listener or lead to misunderstanding.
	• Some pausing while searching for vocabulary but this does not put a strain on the listener.
	• A limited number of cohesive devices are used to indicate the links between ideas.
3 B2.1	• On topic. <u>Presents</u> a coherent message.
	• Incorporates <u>at least half</u> of the information points in the poster into the presentation, giving reasons in support of or against a particular point of view and giving the advantages and disadvantages of various options.
	• Some complex grammar constructions used accurately. Errors do not lead to misunderstanding.
	• Sufficient range of vocabulary to discuss the topic of the poster, and to use synonyms and paraphrase to present some of the information in the poster in his/her own words. When vocabulary is borrowed from the poster, it is used appropriately. Inappropriate lexical choices do not lead to misunderstanding.
	• Pronunciation is intelligible. Mispronunciations do not put a strain on the listener or lead to misunderstanding.
	• Some pausing while searching for vocabulary but this does not put a strain on the listener.
	• A limited number of cohesive devices are used to indicate the links between ideas.
2 B1.2	• Not fully on topic and/or:
	• Presentation limited to a series of linear points describing the information in the poster. <u>Incorporates most of the information points into the presentation, but without providing sufficient reasons or further explanation.</u>
	• Control of simple grammatical structures. Errors occur when attempting complex structures.
	• Limitations in vocabulary make it difficult to deal fully with the task. Relies on the vocabulary provided in the poster to describe the information points. Use of vocabulary borrowed from the poster not always appropriate.

	• Pronunciation is intelligible but occasional mispronunciations put an occasional strain on the listener. • Noticeable pausing, false starts, reformulations and repetition. • Uses only simple cohesive devises. Links between ideas are not always clearly indicated.
1 B1.1	• Not fully on topic and/or: • Presentation limited to a series of linear points describing the information in the poster. <u>Only incorporates some of the information points into the presentation, and does not provide reasons or further explanation.</u> • Control of simple grammatical structures. Errors occur when attempting complex structures. • Limitations in vocabulary make it difficult to deal fully with the task. Relies on the vocabulary provided in the poster to describe the information points. Use of vocabulary borrowed from the poster not always appropriate. • Pronunciation is intelligible but occasional mispronunciations put an occasional strain on the listener. • Noticeable pausing, false starts, reformulations and repetition. • Uses only simple cohesive devises. Links between ideas are not always clearly indicated.
0 A1/A2	• Performance not sufficient for B1, or no meaningful language, or the responses are completely off-topic (memorised or guessing).

Appendix C.1: Click and Drag Item – Norwegian National Testing of English (NNTE) (Reading, 5th Grade)

© Norwegian Directorate for Education and Training (*Utdanningsdirektoratet*)

Appendix C.2: Click and Drag Item – Norwegian National Testing of English (NNTE) (Reading, 5th Grade)

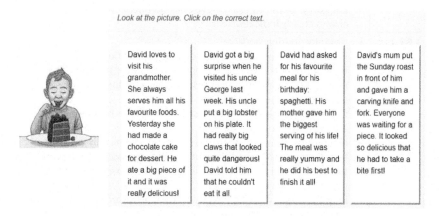

Look at the picture. Click on the correct text.

David loves to visit his grandmother. She always serves him all his favourite foods. Yesterday she had made a chocolate cake for dessert. He ate a big piece of it and it was really delicious!	David got a big surprise when he visited his uncle George last week. His uncle put a big lobster on his plate. It had really big claws that looked quite dangerous! David told him that he couldn't eat it all.	David had asked for his favourite meal for his birthday: spaghetti. His mother gave him the biggest serving of his life! The meal was really yummy and he did his best to finish it all!	David's mum put the Sunday roast in front of him and gave him a carving knife and fork. Everyone was waiting for a piece. It looked so delicious that he had to take a bite first!

© Norwegian Directorate for Education and Training (*Utdanningsdirektoratet*)

Appendix C.3: Aptis for Teens B1 Reading

Appendix C.4: Aptis for Teens B2 Reading

Appendix C.5: Teens Writing Tasks Sample Item

Teens Writing Tasks Sample Item

NB: All items in *italics* change with each new item to follow the theme.

Task 1

> Make friends from around the world with *Global friends*. It's simple to join and fun to use. Fill in the form.
>
> | | |
> |---|---|
> | 1. Your name | |
> | 2. Your date of birth | |
> | 3. Your country | |
> | 4. Your first language | |
> | 5. Your favourite *places*. List 3 | |
>
> Now click on the button to go to step two. [button]

Task 2

> Tell the other members something about yourself. Fill in the form. Write in sentences. Use 20-30 words.
>
> | | |
> |---|---|
> | 1. Personal Information | What do you normally do with *your friends*? |
> | 2. Preferences | Which do you prefer *cars or trains*? Why? |
> | 3. Opinions | What do you think about *homework*? |
>
> Click on the button to register [button]

Task 3

Welcome to *Global friends*. Use our forum to meet other Teens from around the world.

Miguel from Spain has posted this photo on the forum. Add a comment and then reply to two comments from other members. Use 20-30 words for each comment.

Miguel (Spain): *I took this photo at the annual La Tomatina festival in Valencia, Spain. It's really crazy but lots of fun. Would you like to take part in a tomato fight? Why/Why not?*

You:

_____

_____

_____ [post]

Chie (Japan): *I don't think I'd like it. My mum made me eat tomatoes when I was a little kid and now I can't stand them ;-) Has anybody else got a food hate like me?*

You:

_____

_____

_____ [post]

Sandra (Colombia): *I'd love to have a go! I love doing crazy things. Last summer I went surfing. What kind of extreme sports can you do in your country?*

You:

_____

_____

_____ [post]

Task 4

Every month we run a competition on our website. Why not enter? You might win one of our fabulous prizes! The theme this month is *'Global Issues'*. Write your argument in response to this statement. *'There is no need to recycle or use alternative sources of energy as it will make no difference to global warming.'* Remember to include an introduction and a conclusion.

Write your competition entry in 220-250 words here.

Appendix C.6: Aptis General (Adults) B2 Speaking (Long-turn)

Appendix C.7: Aptis for Teens B2 Speaking (Long-turn)

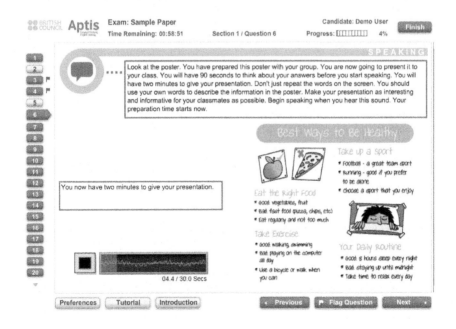

Index

158 *Assessing the Language of Young Learners*

Lightning Source UK Ltd.
Milton Keynes UK
UKOW05f0854030317
295789UK00002B/98/P